THE SECRET OF KIT CAVENAUGH

Christian 'Kit' Cavenaugh, born in 1667 in Dublin, grew up on a Leixlip farm. A dragoon in the Marlborough Wars, Kit led an adventurous life, courting women, fighting duels and arguing a paternity suit before the truth became known: Kit was a woman. After her husband and father of her three children was press-ganged into the English army to fight in the European wars of the early eighteenth century, Kit disguised herself as a man and enlisted to find him. When she finally came face to face with him in 1704, she was enraged to find him in the arms of a Dutch woman. Kit's adventures did not end there . . .

ANNE HOLLAND

THE SECRET OF KIT CAVENAUGH

A Remarkable Irishwoman and Soldier

Complete and Unabridged

ULVERSCROFT
Leicester

First published in Great Britain in 2013 by
The Collins Press
Cork

First Large Print Edition
published 2015
by arrangement with
The Collins Press
Cork

For full details of the Appendix, Bibliography and
Index, please refer to the standard print edition of
this title published by The Collins Press.

ISBN 978–1–4448–2255–7

Published by
F. A. Thorpe (Publishing)
Anstey, Leicestershire

Set by Words & Graphics Ltd.
Anstey, Leicestershire
Printed and bound in Great Britain by
T. J. International Ltd., Padstow, Cornwall

This book is printed on acid-free paper

Contents

Preface

During a visit to the Royal Scots Dragoon Guards museum in Edinburgh Castle, I saw a small item on display referring to 'Mother Ross', a woman who had enlisted as a soldier in order to search for her press-ganged husband. Subsequently, she was wounded three times while serving as a soldier before her sex was discovered, and that set my mind ticking 'story'. Further research included reading a book in Oxford's Bodleian Library, originally published in 1740 and purportedly written by Mother Ross (Kit Cavenaugh) herself. Here indeed was a story of adventure, danger, villainy; jealousy, love, human frailty and heartbreak, and it provides the main source for this book.

During the course of my research, I have visited the site of the Battle of the Boyne a few times, sailed to Williamstadt (where Kit landed), and retraced the full 250 miles of the Long March across the Low Countries, over the Rhine and Moselle, through the mountains, on to the Danube and the little village of Blenheim (Blindheim); although driving along the autobahn in a thunderstorm, lashing rain, lightning and intimidating juggernauts left me thinking the march, from dawn till 9 a.m. each day, then free time, was almost more attractive.

This was back in the 1990s when I inveigled a friend, Sue, to join me. At Hochstadt we were given a private viewing of a detailed model reconstruction of the battle, and at Tapfheim we climbed the church tower from where Marlborough and Prince Eugene had viewed the field of the impending battle. We also visited the battle sites of Ramillies, Oudenarde and Malplaquet, most of them now, like Blenheim itself, just farmland. I also visited Blenheim Palace, where the tapestries convey contemporary pictorial records of the battle; old ships at Portsmouth; the archives of the National Army Museum, London; and the Victoria & Albert Museum in London.

Some reports say Mother Ross was interred in the burial ground of London's Chelsea Hospital with military honours; others, that it was more likely to have been at St Margaret's, Westminster. According to Christine Reynolds of Westminster Abbey Library, the latter was not her final resting place. I have also seen the written entry of her admission to Chelsea from the War Office records held in the National Archives at Kew, courtesy of Alastair Massie of the National

Army Museum. Page 289 records: 'Grant of Chelsea pension to woman who served as soldier within Flanders, 1717.' G.R. Gleig in 1838 quoted her admission from a 'list of old admissions into Chelsea Hospital' as '19 November, 1717. Stair's Dragoons, Catherine Welsh, a fat jolly-breast woman, received several wounds in the service, in the habit of a man; from 19 July 1717.'

It has been said that her account may have been written by Daniel Defoe but this seems unlikely, and the claim has been questioned by, amongst others, Dianne Dugaw, who supplied the entry on her in the *Oxford Dictionary of National Biography*. The story of Kit Cavenaugh is an unusual yarn and it is quite possible, indeed probable, that she herself had a vivid imagination, and there are a number of anomalies in her text, but we do know that her tale is based on fact. Laugh with her, weep for her, love her — or not — this is her story, and I hope you will enjoy reading about her adventurous life as much as I have been absorbed in writing it.

This is a story of actual events written in the creative non-fiction style. There are no fictional characters in the book and direct speech is taken either directly, or adapted, from the memoir published in 1740 of Kit's life, or by using plausible conjecture relevant to a given scene. Scenes are dramatised using settings, personal gestures, and internal thoughts of characters. Details of clothing, military training and so on are described from contemporary records.

A.H.
2013

Acknowledgements

I would like to acknowledge the help of so many supportive people, not least my publisher The Collins Press for enabling me to fulfil my dream of writing this story; thanks to Sue Parrish who has urged me to do it ever since that memorable trip together across Europe, retracing the Long March. I owe particular thanks to James Faulkner; and to the following individuals and institutions:

Blenheim (Blindheim) Museum, Hochstadt; the Bodleian Library, University of Oxford; the Brazen Head, Dublin; Turtle Bunbury; Laura Card, Christine Reynolds and Mark Smith of the Royal Hospital, Chelsea; John Colgan; Grattan de Courcy Wheeler; Colonel Charles Delamain; Patricia Donohue; Dianne Dugaw; Major J. M. K. Erskine; John Gibney; Peter Gibson; Theresa Harris; the Battle of the Boyne Visitor Centre, Oldbridge, County Meath; Ruth Illingworth; Irish Writers' Union; Morgan Llewellyn; Michael McCann; Major Robin Maclean of the Scot's Grey's Museum, Edinburgh Castle; Alastair Massie of the National Army Museum, Chelsea; Ita O'Driscoll; Jane

Ohlmeyer; Royal Scots Dragoon Guards Museum; Dr Chris Scott; Patsy Smiles; Tony Stapleton; The Tyrone Guthrie Centre; and the Westmeath County Council Arts Office.

PART I

1

The Tomboy

'Do that again!'

Kit looked up, startled, quickly pulled her skirt around her, and gasped at the sight above.

She and her four friends had been somersaulting down the lush green hill, giggling and as skittish as wild young colts at play. They had not noticed the nobleman watching from the road above. His coach was drawn by six magnificent grey horses, and his coat of arms was embossed on the side. But it was at the horses that Kit looked, mesmerised.

'Do you hear me? I say do it again!'

He saw them hesitate.

'I'll give you money.'

Kit looked at the earl. His clothes were colourful and expensively cut, and he wore a shoulder-length wig. He had had a bird's-eye view, and he wanted a repeat performance, bare bottoms and all.

'How much?' Kit called.

'Half a crown.'

The girls conferred. Still they were undecided. The youngest started to walk away, thinking the showing of their backsides indecent; others were probably afraid that they might offend the nobleman. Did Kit urge them to do it again for the cash? Quite probably, for we shall see that her love of money was central to her character. One of Kit's friends urged propriety.

'Don't do it again, Kit,' she pleaded, 'he'll see us. Come on.'

But Kit tossed her hair and looked sidelong at the nobleman. No amount of finery would — could — make this man handsome, but Kit was looking beyond him at his six horses. All of them were grey — pure white really — and they *were* handsome.

★ ★ ★

Kit had, unusually, been well educated: 'my parents were both very tender of me, and spared no cost in my education.' She could read proficiently and was an able seamstress, but while Kit's friends were probably demurely learning to spin and weave, earning good money from woollen goods, Kit preferred to tend the sheep that produced the wool.

The word 'tomboy' could have been

invented for Kit. She loved nothing more than to tramp on the moor, to ride, or to work on the farm near the village of Leixlip, with its medieval castle and Protestant church, ten miles west of Dublin. She would guide the plough or wield a flail or pitchfork with, in her words, as much if not more strength and dexterity than any of her mother's servants. She shepherded the flock, checked none were injured or flyblown — and doubtless treated them better than any of the servants if they were. Good farmhands were scarce. Kit relished the challenge of rebuilding the dairy herd after last year's dread disease, of nurturing the land that grew the corn, and of riding around the country-side on her father's horses.

* * *

Kit ignored the other girls' pleadings. Avarice overtook modesty.

'Make it a crown!' Kit looked directly at the nobleman.

She saw him waver. 'Do you want us to do it?'

He chucked down a crown and Kit stooped to pick up the newly minted coin bearing the date of 1685. 'One for each of us!'

He agreed and the girls repeated their

performance, some against their will, but for Kit it was with carefree abandon. All she felt was the warmth of the sun against her body, the rush of blood to her head, and the thrill of increasing speed as she neared the bottom of the hill, with the smell of the summer grass and wild thyme that was released by their cavorting.

The nobleman kept his word and threw the remaining crowns over the hedge, to land at the girls' feet on the hill below him.

Stories like this abound in *The Life and Adventures of Mrs Christian Davies, commonly call'd Mother Ross*, published in 1740, a year after her death.

Christian — Kit — was born in Dublin in 1667, seven years after the Restoration of the monarchy, one year after the Great Fire of London, and 21 years before the Glorious Revolution that was to affect her life so drastically.

★   ★   ★

Kit ran for home, all the while whooping with joy as she imagined she was galloping on one of those magnificent grey beasts. She loved the freedom and the speed as her slender legs carried her effortlessly down the narrow road. It was flanked on both sides by high banks.

On one side a flock of sheep was grazing in the field that led down to the willow-lined brook, the River Rye, while on the other the corn was ripening.

★ ★ ★

Kit, her body as lithe as a youth's, knew she should be more ladylike. She tried to be, for her mother's sake. But after an hour of struggling with needle and thread, or practising her chords, she always slipped out to the farm again. Anyway, she told herself, Mother needs my help out there with Father away in Dublin all week. He rented the farm off Arthur Whyte, whose family owned Leixlip Castle, for £80 a year, which his wife managed 'with great prudence and economy'.

Kit's family lived in what was probably a substantial farmhouse, believed to be on the hill above the village, close to where the Royal Canal now carves its way through the countryside. If the farmhouse was typical of the time, then Kit, returning from her high jinks, would have run through an entrance flanked by stone pillars and down a tree-lined drive elated, probably breathlessly clutching her crown. Around the corner stood the square-set stone farmhouse with its grey slate roof, big chimneys and leaded windows. She paused outside to rinse her hands in the stone water trough fed by a tiny brook. She loved listening to the water bubbling over the stones when she lay quietly in her chamber at night.

Across the yard from the house were the stables and the cow byre, their aroma adding pungency to the warm summer evening. She turned towards the oak front door and breezed into the cool stone farmhouse, straightening her hair and skirt with one smooth, practised sweep, already forgetting the nobleman, but not his magnificent horses.

'Mother!' She knew she'd find her mother in the study, sitting in the creaking, leather-bound chair at her desk, a pile of farm papers in front of her. 'I think we'll be able to cut the oats by the sheep next week, if this weather holds. It's shaping up nicely.'

Mrs Cavanaugh turned slowly and looked at her daughter.

'What *have* you been up to? You look more dishevelled than usual. Go and see what the maid's preparing in the kitchen, will you, dear? I don't want to be too late eating tonight, your father's coming home and bringing a guest with him. And check the spare chamber's been made up ready.'

It took a lot to fluster Kit's mother, but Kit knew something was wrong now. Her grey hair was pinned back neatly as usual, and her plain, full-skirted grey linen dress was clean and crisply pressed, the white lace collar and cuffs being its only concession to prettiness. If anything, her deepening wrinkles increased the pleasantness of her normally rosy-cheeked face. But now it was pale and drawn.

During the week Kit's father ran a successful brewery in the centre of Dublin, close to the various new merchants' halls.

Dublin had several hundred breweries producing a variety of beers for the 1,500 or so ale houses and taverns that served a population of over 50,000. Kit's father worked hard and made a good living, employing some 20 servants; Kit described him as 'remarkable for industry and vigilance in his affairs'.

She may have enjoyed occasional trips into Dublin with him; certainly she was to display a sharp business acumen in later life. She admired her parents, and wrote that through their probity they were highly respected by those around them, a respect which 'they had no claim to from their birth'. They were to imbue their daughter with their work ethic, but never rid her of her sense of adventure. Their Christian names are unknown; Kit never mentions them. We do know, however, that the nearby Confey graveyard includes a John and Edward Cavanagh, and there is another headstone in nearby Kilcock in memory of Charles and Mary Cavanagh, who died in 1715.

In spite of her parents' example of hard work and upright behaviour, Kit could not resist behaving in an unladylike manner, none more so than when it came to riding horses. She would jump up onto them and ride them bareback around the fields, jumping hedges and ditches as she galloped.

There was one particularly fine and fiery horse that no other girl would venture near, which made Kit show off to her friends all the more. No one else could catch him, for he would gallop and dart this way and that, but Kit, with a few oats or a piece of bread in her hand to persuade him, had often done so. She would slip a bridle over his head, stand him in a ditch and from her vantage point on the bank would vault on to his back. Sometimes she would saddle him up and draw and snap pistols, and often 'made my friends apprehend for my life'. She would ride for miles, galloping and jumping across the farm, and doubtless rode along the banks of the Rye to the Liffey. There, she might pause and ponder the mighty 16-foot salmon leap (now submerged to create a 100-acre lake for generating electricity) from which Leixlip gets its name.

Kit might cross the dark, deep river by an old stone bridge that was humpbacked and just wide enough to take a cart, little tufts of grass growing in the middle. She might pull up and peer over the parapet into the deep, still pool, and then look beyond it to where outcrops of rocks caused the water to tumble and surf on its way to Dublin and the sea. Sometimes, when her eyes had adjusted, she could see trout in the pool, almost stationary, their mouths opening and closing in steady rhythm. In autumn she would have seen the salmon leaping up the waterfall as the white water tumbled down over them. Beyond the bridge there was a grassy bank between clumps of gorse and sometimes Kit might sit there for a while in the sunshine, eating a hunk of bread and letting her horse nibble at the short, sweet grass. Sometimes she may have dropped a piece of bread into the water and watched, mesmerised, as the smooth surface boiled over with ripples as shoals of tiny fish vied with each other over the unexpected manna.

One day, she took a grey mare that her grandfather had given to her brother (the only time he is mentioned, and we do not know whether she had other siblings) and, tempted as usual to jump whatever obstacle lay in her way, she 'took a terrible fall' in a dry ditch and injured the mare. One of the farmhands witnessed it, and to keep it a secret from her father she was obliged to buy him a cup of ale every night for a considerable time.

★　★　★

The crop had ripened and Kit was stacking wheat on top of a pile 'near 54 foot high', giving her a view of the surrounding countryside. It was August 1685. Leixlip was nestled at the bottom of the hill and in the distance she would have been able to see the spire of the church in Lucan, the two villages linked by the River Liffey. She paused to wind a kerchief around her mouth and nose to protect them from the dust. It was a long, hot summer and the grain was coming off well.

Below her, to the right of the stack, her mother was one of a group of women binding the corn into stooks, bent low so the fronts of their skirts skimmed the dusty ground. Like this, her mother could have been just one of the workers, instead of their conscientious and prudent employer. The men pitched the stooks up to Kit on top of the stack. It was imperative to get in the crop before it was ruined by rain. But a distant drumming caught Kit's ears, like a roll of thunder. It went again, a steady beat, and this time Kit caught a flash of steel in the sunlight. From her vantage point she was the first to see the men cresting the brow of the hill.

First came bobbing, splendidly bewigged heads, and then a splash of gold and silver coats as they rose further into view. She saw their horses sending out a cloud of dust behind them, their necks arched and their heads held high. They jogged rhythmically in time to the music, tossing their manes, alive and on their mettle. The riders were as fine as any she had ever seen. The martial music stirred Kit's blood and her imagination. One can picture her waving an imaginary musket in the air, longing to be down there with them astride a noble steed. There were noblemen and esquires, all in their finest clothes, with bright red frock coats dripping with gold-braided trimmings and ermine collars and cuffs. At their head, on a sturdy, dapple-grey horse, was the drummer. The trumpeter, astride a bright chestnut horse with flaxen mane and tail, added to the rousing cacophony with notes so high and clear that they willed anyone who could hear them to listen and take note of their chief crier, whose words were echoed by the noblemen in chorus.

'King James!' they proclaimed.

Caught up in the excitement, Kit leapt down from the stack and ran towards them. She jumped over a five-barred gate, calling to her mother as she ran, imagining 'every man there at least a prince'.

Only when she reached the roadside did Kit notice that her mother, instead of lining the route with the rest of the workers and joining in their cheers, was walking swiftly in the opposite direction towards their home, her head bowed and her shoulders stooped as she cried floods of tears. She 'went back and wept bitterly for some time, but would never tell me the reason for her tears'.

2

Sickles and Scythes

Three short years later, the new king was deposed.

At first, Mrs Cavenaugh's fears had appeared unfounded. Ireland seemed stable and prosperous, but the reign of a Catholic king had made Protestants in both Ireland and England uneasy. He was seen as a potential saviour by many of Ireland's Catholics, especially those who had been dispossessed of their land, and who felt that James might yet restore them to what they had lost. His viceroy Richard Talbot, earl of Tyrconnell, began slowly but surely to strip Protestants of their positions in the army and government, replacing them with Catholics. But all this began to change in 1688, when matters came to a head in England, and James's rule ended, thanks to the 'Glorious Revolution'; his English subjects made clear their distaste for his rule and James, facing the reality of his unpopularity, fled to France. His Dutch Protestant son-in-law, William of Orange, ultimately took the English throne, and a Protestant dynasty was restored.

But on 12 March 1689 James landed at Kinsale, having been encouraged by the French to return to Ireland to fight for his three kingdoms. Ireland found itself giving refuge to the English monarch who was still technically its king. James's arrival split loyalties across Ireland: it terrified most of his Protestant subjects and gave heart to his Catholic ones. More and more people began voicing their concerns, and even taking sides. Sometimes the restlessness and unease spilled over into something more than just marching round menacingly, chanting and waving pitchforks, as Kit was to discover.

★ ★ ★

One can imagine the scene and sense of shock when Mr Cavenaugh made a certain announcement to his family.

The meal that night was probably a subdued, tense affair. A hog roasted over a desultory fire and the smell of its juices, as they dripped into the pan beneath, failed to whet the appetites of those around the long oak refectory table. Conversation was formal and stilted, and a weight seemed to lie over the usually light-hearted household.

After the meal Mr Cavenaugh called his

family around him in the study. A flame in the fire flickered and died, as if to draw attention to the speaker. Mrs Cavenaugh sat in a leather-bound chair, while Kit sat on a wooden stool, her brother standing behind her. The spinet, with its 61 notes of ebony and ivory, stood neglected in one corner, by the casement window. No one would be playing it tonight. Mr Cavenaugh stood at his wife's side, one hand resting on her shoulder, and faced his children.

He went straight to the point.

'I am throwing my lot in with James,' he announced. A log in the fire hissed, sending a spit on to the floor that Kit quickly put out with her heel, but not before it had singed the edge of the mat, making Mrs Cavenaugh wrinkle her nose. Otherwise her face, drawn and pale, remained expressionless as her husband continued to speak.

'I'm raising a troop of horse.'

'But father, we're Protestants and he's . . . '

Mr Cavenaugh drew himself up to his full height. 'My daughter, for once I don't care. It is James, and James only in the last several hundred years, who has treated this country fairly.

'You don't remember the horrors of Cromwell's time, but many of us do. It was through him that your mother's parents settled here, but that doesn't mean I'm happy about what his Puritans did to this country and its people, Papist and Protestant.

'No, William of Orange can make all the promises he likes of how he will help us but I, for one, don't believe him. We've heard it all before, and of them all, only James kept his word.

'He deserves our loyalty in return, and if we don't give it to him Dublin will be lost and much more besides.'

Until now the conflict had little affected their lives. The farm was thriving. Hearsay concerning William's ambitions was one thing, but now the family was suddenly becoming embroiled in the war that was on the verge of erupting.

Mrs Cavenaugh, as ever, said very little. But her face gave away many of her thoughts. Her cheeks were wrinkled, worry lines furrowed her brow, and her eyes were dull, almost misted.

Mr Cavenaugh continued. 'I'll be taking our best horse for my own personal use.'

At this, Kit could not prevent a gasp. That was her favourite horse. She covered her mouth with her hand and continued to listen.

'Kit, I want you to look after your mother and help on the farm . . . '

'I do already.'

'Don't be impertinent. You've been lucky enough to have a better education than most young women. Don't waste it. Oh, and by the way, I'm also taking the cowherd with me, you'll have to do most of the milking from now on.'

Kit records that the Irish 'very readily' espoused James's cause, and her father's conscience told him it was 'incumbent on him to support his lawful sovereign, notwithstanding his being of a different religion, which he thought not sufficient reason to affect his loyalty'.

★   ★   ★

Now her father, the cowherd, and many of the other able-bodied men were gone, as were the sons and servants of neighbouring farmers. So too were their horses, all gone to join Cavenaugh's troop in support of King James.

Battle could not be far away, and tension spread. One morning, Kit wandered up to the cornfields after milking; she would check on the state of the harvest before helping her mother indoors by sewing together grey jackets suitable for battle.

The countryside looked and smelled beautiful. God, she loved it. It seemed a cruel irony that the country was being thrown into war, on behalf of the rightful king.

An old hound bitch rubbed up against her leg while Kit paused, listening to the skylark. It was a beautiful summer's day. A group of sparrows that had been picking up bits of food at the edge of the rough road rose up, scattering dust behind them, at the approach of Kit and the hound, now rather slow and lame.

As she neared the wheat field Kit heard an extraordinary noise. Men were yelling, metal was clanging, and all appeared to be in uproar. On the crest of the hill, Kit was confronted by what appeared to be a pitched battle. Workmen — boys too young to join up and men too old — from the neighbouring farm and hers were slashing at each other with their sickles. Blood and frayed clothing were everywhere, and the men uttered blood-curdling yells, like battle cries.

'Get off our land, I tell you!'

'It's not yours, it's ours!'

'You're stealing!'

'No, you're stealing, you filthy beggars, now get off.' With that an old man who looked much too ancient to be flaying a sickle at corn let alone in anger, struck out again.

A youth ducked and yelled again. 'We're under orders to cut this corn!'

'You're not, you can't be, it's ours . . . '

Just then her mother, having heard the noise, arrived and, with difficulty, called them off. Kit's father had failed to tell his wife that he had sold the corn (in fact, he had done so in order to buy enough good horses and muskets in Dublin for his troop), so she sent their remaining men up to begin harvesting it, only for them to find the neighbour's men already doing so. At length she was able to appease her erstwhile workers, but only after regaling them with 'a good breakfast and strong liquors'.

Keeping control of the farm was going to be tougher than Kit had thought.

★ ★ ★

'Heave!'

The motley gang did as the sergeant bade, all the while chanting and shouting as they hauled on whatever solid objects they could find with which to block the church door. The peaceful Irish countryside was being filled with scenes of turmoil and distrust, like this one outside the church in Leixlip.

'Pull harder!' the sergeant commanded the men around him as they laboured with massive lengths of lumber. One of them had got hold of a butcher's block, and another

21

was trying to force a plank through the heavy iron latch on the church door, effectively locking it. The men wiped sweat from their foreheads and hauled the timber again.

The church was now secured, its Protestant congregation locked inside.

★ ★ ★

Mrs Cavenaugh was inside the whitewashed church with its plain glass nave windows. It was built along simple Norman lines. A wooden gallery at the rear was supported on each side by plain stone pillars. Perhaps Mrs Cavenaugh sat beside the black iron plaque in the wall erected by Lady Ursula Whyte in memory of her husband, who had died in 1654, and one of her sons, Nicholas, who had died ten years later; she was the mother of the Cavenaugh's landlord, Arthur Whyte. The sermon would probably last an hour and was unlikely to be alleviated by hymns, which were generally sung in private houses. Perhaps her mind wandered: was it true that Robert the Bruce and his horses had sought refuge in this very church? And was there really an underground tunnel leading from it to nearby Leixlip Castle?

A commotion outside shattered such reveries. For a moment the vicar, the Rev.

Mallory, continued, but raised voices and the sound of heavy objects banging against the door stopped him short.

⋆　⋆　⋆

Kit was in the house but heard the noise and, fearing for the safety of her mother, she snatched up a spit, ran to the scene and tried to force her way through.

'How dare you!' Kit yelled. Almost blind with fury, she shoved her way past the bystanders, cutting a path through the mob by the swing of her spit.

'Detain that woman!' the sergeant ordered.

Kit, in a fury, stopped waving the spit and thrust it instead straight into the sergeant's calf. As the rest looked on in horror she strode up to the church door, knocked free the restraining lumber, unlatched the door and marched in. Coolly, Kit called out to her mother.

'Dinner's ready, Mother. Come now.'

The sergeant stood on the threshold, holding his leg and looking murderous. A number of people received minor injuries in the ensuing scuffle, including the Rev. Mallory, the minister, as the congregation escaped the mob and dispersed in the village. But not Kit. The sergeant caught hold of her and pulled her towards him.

'You're coming before the magistrate,' he said through gritted teeth, 'now.'

Limping, he led her towards the court-house.

★ ★ ★

Kit stood in the dock of the courtroom, the wooden rail in front of her worn where previous occupants had clenched it. There was a chill feel to the dank, gloomy room, and a vague smell of polish. The sergeant remained beside her. A small group of people who had followed them sat in the public gallery.

'Pay attention. Court rise,' the usher demanded as the magistrate swept in and took his seat.

Kit held her head up high, threw back her shoulders and spoke in a clear voice in answer to the charge of assault. 'Not guilty, my lord.'

Kit's account does not tell us what happened in the courtroom beyond her representing the hardship of her mother being interrupted in her worship, when her 'father was actually in arms for the service of the prince for whom they pretended great zeal'. Their actions, she said, 'alienated the hearts of his subjects, and gave ground to his enemies to raise a clamour'.

The case against her was dismissed and she was acquitted.

3

The Battle of the Boyne

The great River Boyne flowed languidly through Oldbridge, a few miles upstream from Drogheda. For William it was now the only barrier between him and Dublin.

The river was tidal at this point, and teemed with fish. James's army of 23,000 guarded a fording point near Oldbridge. A little further south the river reached Rosnarce before turning north again to Slane, where, as part of the battle preparations the Jacobites had destroyed the bridge to prevent their enemy crossing it. But the possibility remained that James's army could be outflanked if their opponents marched upstream and managed to ford the river somewhere else. If that happened, their only escape route would be by bridge over the Nanny, a tributary of the Boyne at Duleek.

William's larger army was encamped on high ground north of the river at Tullyallen, affording them fine views of what would soon become a battlefield. His men were awake and drilled and each had consumed his generous ration of brandy. Alert and ready, all they awaited now was the fanfare to signal the start of battle. It was Tuesday, 1 July 1690.

★ ★ ★

James was more nervous than he had ever been before. He was elderly, and he was to fight his son-in-law. Men as old as him, like Cavenaugh, had raised troops to rally to his cause. There were others who had advised him to return to France; but James did not want to relinquish control tamely of the last of what had once been his three kingdoms.

At a pre-dawn breakfast in Donore, overlooking the river, he had summoned his leaders to discuss the battle plans.

James had not wanted this imminent confrontation. He would have wanted it even less had he known about the gaming and drinking that had kept many of his men up most of the night, or that many of them wore ragged clothing and carried inadequate arms. Across the river he would have seen plainly the lines of William's troops. And what James could not see for himself, his spies reported back to him. It was not what he wanted to hear: an army of 36,000, equipped with the most up-to-date muskets, while the Dutch and Danish forces assisting had bayonets; a well-supplied hospital was in readiness at their rear, with first-aid posts scattered through the camp (apparently one of the first times such facilities were deployed on a battlefield). And there was no shortage of food: some 550 wagonloads of supplies, 2,500 draught horses and an artillery train had all been ferried across the Irish Sea. William himself held authority in a portable wooden house designed for him by Christopher Wren, from where he issued orders, dined in luxury and slept in comfort.

Scouts from both sides had galloped back and forth, garnering knowledge of the enemy. One of the Williamites, Colonel Robert Byerley, got too close to James's guards and was almost captured; he had had to spur the horse to full speed to escape. But there was a postscript: his horse, the 'Byerley Turk', later became the first of the three progenitors of the thoroughbred racehorse; he contested and is believed to have won a race at Down Royal before serving here in the Battle of the Boyne.

There had been no battle the previous day because a Monday was considered unlucky, or, as one Williamite put it, 'the day being a Monday on which the King never undertakes anything of importance'. However, plenty of sniper fire had been exchanged. William was out on his horse assessing the Jacobite lines when a cannon shot rang out across the river and grazed his shoulder. William, on a white horse, had perhaps been too easy to spot. Reports reached James that the enemy leader was dead; James might find himself restored to the English throne (and the whole course of Irish history altered) without a fight at all. Much whispering ensued but finally, conclusive proof arrived that William was alive. He had reportedly quipped of the close encounter, 'It was as well it came no closer.'

★　★　★

Now, in the misty first light, a messenger galloped up to James and told him that the enemy was on the point of attack. They had sent a force two miles upstream to ford the river; it looked like nearly a third of their whole army, which would leave James's left flank vulnerable.

As if on cue, the mist cleared. The drums rolled and the bugles sounded their fanfare. The summer sun shone and the battle began.

★　★　★

With the mist gone two stark images struck James. He could see the main thrust of William's army heading straight down the far side bank towards him but there, in the distance, he made out a column of men marching upstream. If they reached Rosnaree they would be able to ford the river. He despatched 800 dragoons under Sir Neal O'Neal to intercept them.

Directly ahead of James, the Williamite infantry were discharging their flintlocks in continuous volleys. By contrast, his own men's matchlock muskets were hopelessly inadequate; some did not work, and those that did were fatally slow. They could fire only three shots per minute, and in the agonising seconds between each reloading, the gunners had only pikemen to defend them. All the time William's massed ranks, bearing green sprigs in their hats, made a full frontal attack. The Jacobites fought bravely. Bodies lay strewn along the banks of the river, but mostly on James's side. Acrid smoke hung in a pall over all of them.

★   ★   ★

In Leixlip, Kit could not have known of the battle, but must have heard rumours. Perhaps she paused from milking the cows and stretched her back. She would have wondered how her father was faring; not to mention the fate of her precious horse. Doubtless she sent up a silent prayer for his safe return, stooped down again to place the pail beneath the next cow, and rhythmically continued pulling at the teats on the full udder, one hand over the other, up, down, up, down. Trit, trot, trit, trot; perhaps she imagined herself riding across the farm, heading for the Liffey, cantering, or jumping a fallen tree.

'Ouch!' The cow, long emptied of her milk, kicked Kit on her thigh in protest, jolting her out of her reverie. She must pour the milk into the churn, push the handcart up to the road, and hope that someone from the creamery would collect it today.

★ ★ ★

'Charge!'

The 800 Jacobite dragoons deployed upriver obeyed Sir Neal O'Neill. Vigorously they defended the ford at Rosnaree, successfully resisting the Williamite attempts to cross it. The clash of steel and gunpowder smoke filled the air. A shell whizzed through the air and hit Sir Neal, smashing his thigh and rendering him useless; with that, the Jacobite threat at Rosnaree was extinguished. Sir Neal, a Catholic like his king, was the eldest son of Sir Hugh O'Neill of Clandeboy. He died four days later and was buried in Waterford.

James sent a large contingent of reinforcements to stem the Williamite advance but, at a place called Roughgrange, a boggy-bottomed ravine proved to be an impregnable barrier separating the two armies, leaving them at a stand-off for the remainder of the day. James could ill afford to have so many men standing there idle, for in front of him, to his horror, the enemy began wading across the river, waist deep and ten abreast, to face James's vastly depleted army here.

Later, further downstream more were wading through water that was up to their armpits, holding their muskets and powder above their heads as they forced themselves through the current, struggling to keep their balance. As they attempted to deploy on landing they were easy prey for the Jacobite gunners; some Williamites found their powder had got damp, others were shot down before they had time to ready themselves. When the Williamite commander Schomburg was killed the Jacobites were encouraged to fight with renewed vigour, their battle not yet lost.

★ ★ ★

After leaving the milk churn, Kit may have walked to where the sheep were grazing. Shorn now, they would have looked semi-naked. Kit knew she must do some spinning; the wool was a means of earning and besides, the men might want more woollen clothing once they returned. If they returned. She kicked a stone and walked back to the farmhouse, determined to do what she could.

★ ★ ★

For two more hours the fortunes of the battle swung from one side to the other. Further downstream from Oldbridge William, mounted on his distinctive horse, attempted to ford the river at the head of his Dutch Blue Guards and his cavalry, accompanied by the Inniskilling Regiment of Foot (later the Royal Inniskilling Fusiliers). Once safely over they quickly re-formed into a fighting force, charging directly towards the Jacobite right flank. Taken aback by this unexpected onslaught, the Jacobites were steadily depleted.

James was informed that his men were being forced to give way; rather than run the risk of being surrounded and captured, he retreated from the battlefield and left the Williamites to their victory. As news spread that James had abandoned the field, the Jacobite forces soon followed suit.

The Battle of the Boyne was over and

William of Orange had won the day. Two days later he marched triumphantly into Dublin.

*   *   *

Kit's father escaped the rout and galloped for home, accompanied by a handsome young Frenchman, Lieutenant Bordeaux, who appeared to be a trusted confidant of her father. Mrs Cavanaugh received the stranger with civility, ordered the maid to prepare a meal for them, and arranged for the visitor to sleep in Kit's bed. They stayed only until 3 a.m. when, fearing that they were in danger from the Williamites, they fled.

As their horses were being saddled, Mr Cavenaugh gathered his family around him. With tears in his eyes he blessed them, and then turned to his wife.

'Do not be dejected; comfort yourself, that whatever misfortunes befall us, we suffer in a just cause, and for having done what is the duty of every loyal subject; at least, my conscience tells me that I have acted as I ought, and as I was bound to do by my oath of allegiance, from which I know no power on earth that can absolve me. The Lord giveth, and the Lord taketh away, blessed be the name of the Lord. His ways are inscrutable, and I humbly submit to His decrees, which are all founded in wisdom. You, being a Protestant, need apprehend no danger from the enemy. Never torment yourself with uneasy thoughts for your unfortunate husband. Think of me no more.'

'God forbid.' Mrs Cavenaugh burst into floods of tears and her husband, 'who could not bear to see her weep, as he loved her with a sincere tenderness, ran out of the room, and he and the officer mounting their horses, fled with precipitation'.

★   ★   ★

James spent only one night in Dublin after the Battle of the Boyne, then journeyed to Duncannon, the small fortified harbour village in Wexford a few miles from storm-struck Hook Head. As soon as he could he boarded a ship in Kinsale, County Cork, to return him to the safety he sought in France. There, in St Germain, he died of a stroke in 1701, at the age of 66. As for William, he departed Ireland within weeks of his victory at the Boyne. But the war did not end there.

★   ★   ★

The Jacobites had re-formed and continued to fight, Kit's father among them. They

34

eventually retreated to Connacht, hoping that the French would send the troops that could turn the tide against them. But the French had lost interest in the war in Ireland, and in 1691 the Williamite army crossed the River Shannon at Athlone. On 12 July 1691, the two armies faced each other at Aughrim in County Galway, this time without the two kings who had led them at the Boyne.

Kit's father was in the Jacobite ranks, and when battle commenced he and his fellows greeted the Williamites with a hail of fire. But, in a monumental military blunder, the reserve supply of musket balls were the wrong size for the muskets, and the Jacobites, left virtually defenceless, were cut down, left lying like so many dead sheep. The death of the Jacobite commander St Ruth turned the tide further and the remaining Jacobites fled in disarray, to be cut down by the Williamite cavalry that followed them in what remains the bloodiest battle ever fought in Ireland: perhaps 7,000 men lost their lives.

Kit's father was amongst those wounded, but his injuries seem not to have been too serious. Cavenaugh was tended by able surgeons, and appeared to be well on the road to recovery. But the night before he was due to return home, one of the men who had served under him, 'an Irish Papist' called

Kelly, took advantage of his indisposition and the dark night, and ran away with Cavenaugh's horses to join the Williamite army. Kit recorded that 'this villainous ingratitude from a man whom he had always treated with great humanity had such an effect on my father that he was seized with a fever which carried him off in a short time'.

* * *

The war was not yet over, and soon there was to be a discovery that would affect Kit's future life profoundly. The Jacobites retreated to Limerick where they eventually made their last stand. As the Williamites besieged the city, Cavenaugh's French companion, Bordeaux (who was now promoted to captain) commanded a body of troops defending a bridge with, as Kit recorded, 'so much gallantry that he was admired, and his death lamented, by even his enemies who, to their great surprise, found on stripping this brave officer that it was a woman had given such proof of an invincible courage'.

It seems reasonable to suggest that she had been Cavenaugh's mistress, but whatever the reason for her disguise, Kit was to have cause to remember it.

* * *

The Treaty of Limerick brought the war in Ireland to an end in October 1691. Kit's father was dead, but at least the farm was safe thanks to a pardon his wife had obtained; or so they thought. But at some point after the end of the war the cherished pardon was rescinded and the Williamite government seized their property; Kit and her mother were left destitute.

4

That Inestimable Jewell

Kit faced a future of poverty. Worse than that, being penniless meant she could no longer provide a substantial dowry with which to tempt a wealthy suitor, so she would be unable to marry well. She had been both eligible and desirable; now, she felt, she was neither. For Kit, carefree, confident and used to getting her way, the change in fortune was devastating.

By today's standards and terminology, she could be described as having come from a fairly affluent family that had risen to be (for want of a better term) middle class; she was well educated, with good manners, and had not lacked for the material things of life. Her father had been building up his brewery in Dublin at a time when that city was starting to expand into the metropolis it would become in the eighteenth century. The farm, run by Kit and her mother, had also been doing well. Now all seemed lost. Confiscation generally applied to land only, and those who lost land in that way were usually allowed to take their effects with them. If, however, the confiscation also specified goods and chattels, then everything would be taken. And Kit's account recorded that 'the government seized upon all his effects'.

And so it may be the case that Kit's family lost virtually everything except the clothes they stood up in. All their belongings, their furniture and their animals would have been taken; the loss of the latter would have meant that they would be unable to pay the rent due to Whyte, their landlord. If they had owned the house, that would have been taken as well. They may have been able to go 'on the parish', or to rely on the aid of relatives — always assuming that relatives had not suffered the same fate. But virtually all of their possessions were gone.

By now, Kit was 'of age', and she had caught the eye of a young man by the name of Thomas Howell. He was a son of her mother's first cousin, and his uncle was a bishop. Howell was himself a theological student at Trinity College Dublin, and made 'warm love' to Kit by attempting to woo her for the better part of two years. At first she was flattered, believing him to be sincere, and she 'found my esteem for him greater than my concern for my own interest'. But as he became keener, so she began to worry about her lack of fortune, and she 'begged him to stop pursuing her', saying she had nothing except a barrel of brass crowns to bring him, and she would not consent to his ruin. Howell could not see, as Kit put it, 'the evils probably consequential of the completion' of his wishes. 'We easily satisfy ourselves with arguments which flatter our inclinations, however weak,' Kit recorded. 'This was his case; for when I laid before him the certain poverty which would attend his marrying a woman without a fortune he removed the objection.'

Undeterred, he told her he had a bright future in the Church of Ireland — the state church — and could, in the meantime, run a Latin school to earn sufficient funds to keep her like a lady.

Kit countered that it would be deplorable to be a clergyman's widow with, possibly, a number of children.

Unbowed, he asserted, 'my economy will ward against that evil.'

'Bah', she replied, 'that's castles in the air. I cannot consent to you, it would be your undoing and my ruin.'

She begged him to stop pursuing her but to no avail. He continued his 'visits and solicitations', which became 'more frequent, longer and urgent'.

One day, when she was alone in the house and making the beds, he paid yet another visit. In Kit's words, he 'took hold of the opportunity, threw himself at my feet, embraced my knees and urged his suit with such vehemence, such warmth of expression, such tender embraces, such ardent kisses that, finding by my eyes and short breath, I had caught the contagious desire, he added force to vows of eternal constancy and marriage, and, with little resistance on my side, threw me upon the bed, deprived me of that inestimable jewell which a maiden ought to preserve preferable to life.'

Thomas Howell left soon afterwards. Kit straight away 'repented my weakness; and, with sincere tears of penitence, cursed the time, myself, and the undoer; I raved, tore my hair, and was not far from madness'.

By that evening, and with her mother due back, she tried to compose herself 'that I might not betray my folly'. Her mother, however, immediately noticed her swollen eyes and asked her what the matter was. Kit gave only an evasive answer.

She could not sleep that night and 'the remembrance of what had passed had such an effect upon me that I lost both my colour and stomach'.

She could not bear to see any of her friends

and, while normally an outdoor type, she tried to stay out of the sunlight. Her melancholy became so bad that 'everyone took notice of it'. Her mother, 'sensibly touched with this sudden change, often tenderly inquired of me what ground I had for the sadness which gave her so much uneasiness; for she feared so sudden and settled a grief, as was impossible for me to dissemble, would endanger my life'.

No one could coax the troubled story from her. Doubtless worried in case she was pregnant, Kit asked if she could leave home. Her mother readily agreed, hoping a change of air and company might restore her daughter. Kit had an aunt who owned a tavern in Dublin, and it was agreed she would go there.

★   ★   ★

With their horses and carts or carriages gone, it is likely that Kit walked the ten or so miles to the tavern, believed to have been called 'The Pig and Bagpipes'. She probably started off by walking down the hill to the banks of the River Liffey. The great, dark river that had begun its journey high in the Wicklow Mountains, reached its northernmost tip in Leixlip before curling around, almost at a right angle, to flow towards Dublin; it would act as Kit's guide eastwards towards the city. Was her melancholy as dark as the river? Probably, for as yet she did not know whether or not she was with child.

Perhaps she wiped her face with her dress sleeve, likely to have been a plain piece of dull grey cloth that, with her oldest cloak, would be all the clothing she had left. Maybe blisters formed on her feet. She may have stooped down at the river's edge, cupped her hands to take in water, and splashed her face with it. She dangled her feet into the refreshing water, cooling and stinging at the same time.

A wagtail strutted on a rock in the river, its tail bobbing up and down as it looked for insects.

She could see the church spire of Lucan and began to see boats on the river. Shortly afterwards she was confronted by a deep gorge (today spanned by a high bridge carrying the M50 motorway around the city). Beyond it were the buildings of Dublin. She would have passed through the Knockmaroon Gate and skirted the city park: the 1,762-acre Phoenix Park (in Irish, *fionn uisce*, meaning bright water) remains Europe's largest walled inner city park: it was created in 1662 as a royal demesne for hunting deer, five years before Kit's birth.

From her vantage near the park, Kit would have been able to see the outline of the Royal Hospital at Kilmainham, opened only a few years earlier in 1684 for maimed soldiers; little could she have guessed then how a similar institution would become her home in later life.

She soon entered the city itself. The river became wider and bustled with traffic, guarded by buildings skirting the water's edge. Barges were being unloaded with coal (which was gradually taking the place of wood for fires) from England, with wine from France and Spain, and timber from the Baltic. Vessels were probably being loaded with barrels of salt pork and beef in brine, bound for shipment to America, and dairy goods and grain, too. Pork was one of the best meats for travel as it needed less salting and stayed juicy longer; also, every part of the pig could be used: its ears were boiled, sliced and fried, the trotters were pickled, the blood was used in black pudding, and the lard was used for cooking.

Amongst the goods on the docks, there might also have been linen produced nearby at Chapelizod. Beer too, although in the early years of brewing there were no hops in Irish ale, Ireland was by now growing hops. Kit would probably have known the area around the docks through her father; his brewery had drawn its water from the Liffey, but beer would not be exported from Ireland for another century or so.

Kit crossed the river just past Wood Quay, the city already bustling with activity: street criers extolling the virtues of their wares, and a knife grinder pushing his one-wheeled cart (much like a wheelbarrow), and beggars putting out their cupped hands. But Kit kept her head bowed; all that she saw were the vegetable peelings mixed with horse droppings and sewage along the gutter.

There were alehouses everywhere, and Kit probably wondered if she would remember the way to her aunt's tavern amongst so many others. She took the turning into Bridge Street, leading her away from the Liffey and up a steep, cobbled hill lined with rows of black-and-white houses: the gilded key outside one indicated the locksmith's, the candle-maker's wrought-iron sign was coloured brightly in different shapes like candles, and the dress-maker's scissors, in unpainted iron, marked his establishment. She wound her way past Dublin Castle towards Hoggen Green and there ahead of her was Trinity College with its three quadrangles and its park for the fellows' horses; had she gone too far? She trudged back another way, with the Wicklow Mountains now rising to her left in the distance beyond St Stephen's Green, which had been enclosed less than 30 years before Kit's arrival in the city. She walked on to Christ Church Cathedral; could she hear singing from its choir? She probably wasn't listening as she searched for her aunt's tavern, let alone recall that it was this cathedral that housed, legend had it, the tomb of the Norman invader Strong-bow.

There it was. To her right she could see the sign picturing a large pig's head and a set of bagpipes hanging over the entrance to her aunt's inn: The Pig and Bagpipes. The black-and-white building was set back from the road and approached down steep steps with a ramp on the left where the newly arrived barrels of ale were rolled down; the date '1666' was inscribed above the door.

As Kit walked across the uneven flagstones she would have noticed an all-pervading mix of smells, from tobacco smoke and wood ash to the aroma of the local beer. Jugs and pewter mugs hung from hooks above the bar, along with pots of tin and painted earthen-ware, and sack bottles. Wooden settles were placed around the edge of the small, square, low-beamed room. An archway by the bar counter led to the front bar, sawdust was scattered on its floor and a small square window added light to the gloom. A blazing fire, with open sides, heated both rooms. Hooks hung at varying heights above the range, to give different cooking heats. To one side stood an hourglass for timing the cooking, along with a nutmeg grater and a quantity of herbs; while above hung maybe a rabbit or a pheasant. Placed on the trestle was a side of bacon for curing and fruits to dry, conserve or consume fresh, along with piles of vegetables.

★ ★ ★

Kit would soon have started to help with the numerous chores that her aunt undertook before the first customers arrived each day. These would have included going outside into the courtyard to retrieve a barrel of ale from the pile stacked at the foot of the ramp. She would roll it inside, and would then manoeuvre it to the corner of the bar, ready to draw from. Some of the regular customers probably had their own special mugs hanging from the ceiling and she would fill them and hand them over as she saw their owners entering. Then, still breathless from shifting the barrel, she would rake up the ashes and put them in a pail, and then sweep the hearth before taking the pail outside and flinging the ashes on the patch of grass and weeds and mud that formed a back yard leading to a row of stables. From the corner of the yard she might pick up a bundle of kindling wood, drop it into her apron pocket, and then collect armfuls of logs and, cradling her load in front of her like a pregnant woman, pick her way inside. She laid the fire and lit it, and blew on it when the damp wood was slow to take. She then fanned the infant flames with her apron. Satisfied that it was properly alight, she collected her pot of polish and a duster and completed her daily chore of polishing the bar tops, the tables and even the chairs, stools and settles, and window sills and any other piece of wood that looked in the least as if it might need to be cleaned. She sprinkled sawdust on the earthen floor of the front bar, working backwards from the front door to keep her feet clean, and then returned to the kitchen and took out the bread.

The oven was heated by a fire and the cinders were taken out before the dough was placed inside; as usual, the loaves had risen beautifully and would be devoured with pickled eggs by her customers with their usual gusto later on. Next she finished rolling some pastry which she would have prepared earlier, cut it into squares and filled them with cooked potatoes, carrots, onions and mutton, sealed over the pastry, and popped them, two dozen or more, into the hottest part of the range. Her aunt doubtless thought one of those would be good for her niece, whatever it was that troubled her.

* * *

In her distress Kit doubtless still shivered at the thought of that man taking advantage of her. He had deprived her of her virginity. Had it been rape? Please God, she hadn't encouraged him, had she? If so, how would she ever forgive herself? Or face her mother again? She prayed that no one, not least her aunt, would ask prying questions. She would rather take a vow of silence than confess what had happened to her. And again the fear passed through her: supposing she was pregnant?

5

Love and Reason Seldom Agree

Kit threw herself into her new life, presumably still in possession of no more than her 'barrel of brass crowns'. Naturally a hard worker, she strove to banish the memory of what had happened that day, but it was not until a few weeks had gone by and she knew she could not be with child, that she regained a little colour. 'My melancholy, after I found no ill-consequence attend our guilt, began to wear off by degrees and I gradually recovered my colour and cheerfulness of temper.'

At first, Thomas Howell continued to visit, but she refused to see him — she 'carefully avoided allowing him any opportunity of speaking to me, and took such an inveterate hatred to him, that he at last was sensible his pursuit was vain'. Only then did Kit return to something like her old cheerful self. As for men, it seems certain she rebuffed the attentions of most potential suitors, and undoubtedly there were many.

Soon there was no aspect of running the inn at which Kit did not excel, and the business thrived. The picture she paints of herself, though, is at odds with that of her early, carefree life on the farm, for she describes herself as behaving towards her aunt 'with such dutiful respect, observance and vigilance, and with such a reserved yet obliging manner to others that I entirely captivated her good opinion and engaged her tenderness'.

All this paid off when her aunt died and left Kit as sole heiress, leaving her 'in possession of a house well-furnished and well-accustomed'. She now lived 'in ease and plenty'; she 'got money apace and was esteemed by all my neighbours and acquaintance'.

Kit's natural business skills, already honed at home, meant she seamlessly swapped the business of the farm for that of the inn trade. We can imagine her being innovative in the kitchen and canny when out in the early morning down among the traders along the quays, darting from stall to stall on the market days of Wednesday and Saturday, striking the best bargains and bringing back the freshest produce to turn into tempting delicacies. Fresh fish and game would have been readily available, and so she may have served freshly caught trout in jelly with saffron, young fried rabbit in butter with spinach, and potato pancakes. Mackerel, stewed scallops, or smoked eels are also likely to have been on her menu. On All Hallows' Eve, beginning to be known at this time as Hallowe'en, it may have been her apple dumplings and potato cakes or the colcannon; into this mixture of cabbage and potato she would have popped the charms which tradition said would bring fortune to whoever found it in his portion: the ring that would bring marriage within a year, or a coin to indicate riches to come, but the tinder of either the thimble or the button, it was said, would never marry.

On Sundays Kit may have walked to St Catherine's Church; sitting in a high-backed wooden pew she could read the memorial tablet to Henry Duffe, the last abbot of St Thomas Abbey to which this church had been a chapel of ease. During long sermons she let her mind wander. Next to the stone for Duffe was one for the curates appointed by the Crown which took over the newly formed parish of St Catherine's after the Abbey was dissolved under Henry VIII, firstly Sir John Brace, the former prior of the abbey who was succeeded only a short time after by Peter Ledwidge; she mused on what might have happened to Sir John but then the lengthy sermon ended and the congregation stood up, some shuffling slowly erect, others almost leaping upright, and chanted in unison, 'The Lord is my Shepherd.'

Refreshed, she might run back down the hill and within minutes be drawing beer from the tap on the barrel once more.

It is clear from Kit's account that, since her deflowering, she had led an upright and chaste life, spurning all advances from men. All that was to change.

Thanks to her aunt's bequest she had everything she wanted in life, and 'never woman was in a happier situation; for I was at the height of my ambition and had not a wish to make. In a word I was thoroughly content, and had reason so to be, till love, too often the bane of our sex; love, who has not seldom ruined noble families, nay, destroyed cities, and lain kingdoms waste; envious of the calm I enjoyed, came to embitter my peace, disturb the tranquillity of my life, and make me know, by experience, the short duration of all sublunary satisfaction.'

Richard Welsh had been one of her aunt's servants and was now employed by Kit. What triggered the spark between them is unclear, but he now found his way to her heart. Her description of him is glowing. 'He was very well made in his person, had a handsome, manly face; was of a generous, open temper; sober, vigilant, and active in his business, very regular in his life, and modest in his behaviour.'

He was, or appeared to Kit, to be a man 'whom any woman might love without having her good sense called into question'.

In Kit's eyes he was a paragon of virtue. But there was a problem. She was the mistress; he was her servant. Her mother was still alive, and at that time the preservation of a family's good name in marriage was paramount; nothing should be done to diminish it. It was a time when, for instance, a landless labourer was considered untouchable, and no farmer's daughter should be allowed to marry one. To marry into a lower class was to risk disinheritance. Kit, however, was already financially independent.

There was another consideration; it was by no means unusual for all of a woman's property to pass to her husband on marriage. How could Kit risk losing everything through marriage to a servant? At first her pride made her 'stifle my growing passion' which she tried to conquer by reason, telling herself it 'must be to the disadvantage of my fortune'.

Richard Welsh had some savings but this was 'a trifle' compared to what Kit's aunt had left her, and the business was still improving daily.

'But love and reason seldom agree,' she

wrote, 'and when once that despotic tyrant gets possession of the heart, he will also rule the head: my pride and reason made but vain efforts, and he would listen to neither; the more they disputed, the more absolute the little domineerer grew; in a very little time he humbled my haughtiness, and silenced my reason: the sight of Richard Welsh overturned the strongest resolutions that I could make; his name was music to my ears; if I did not see him, no other object could please my eyes and I knew no other happiness but in possession of Richard Welsh.'

There was yet another obstacle. Having vanquished her pride and reason, her modesty made her hold out longer: it would be indecent and a reflection on her sex, she thought, to make the first overture.

So there were restless nights for Kit, yearning for a man who was apparently out of reach. Eventually she confided her feelings to a friend — we'll call her Mary — whom she persuaded to ask Richard to make his advances.

Richard was also in love with his mistress, and for long had held her best interests in his heart. But it was still not as simple as that for, from his point of view, if his advances were spurned — and Kit was well practised in that — he would not only lose his prospects with her but probably also his job as well, as he made clear to Mary when she found a chance to speak with him in private.

She told him that not only was his employer aware of his honesty, hard work and excellent character but also, 'between you and me, friend Richard, I fancy she has a sneaking kindness for you'. She thought it possible that he could become master instead of servant 'if you have the courage to attack . . . remember the proverb, *faint heart never won fair lady.*'

Richard still hesitated.

'I like my mistress very well,' he replied, 'and I have a very good place that I would be loathe to lose, which I'm afraid I would if I was unsuccessful.'

'Believe me, Richard,' Mary replied, 'none of us are displeased at being admired. We may pretend to be angry, but that is a cloak . . . try your fortune with her and, on my life, you carry her.'

★ ★ ★

The next evening Kit probably chose her dress to wear in front of the customers with care. The satin gown set off her hair and complexion beautifully. The rounded neckline was low enough to give a hint of her small breasts tantalisingly just out of sight, the lace frill making her look more buxom than she really was, and the sleeves hugged her slim arms until they opened up into wide cuffs also frilled with lace. Her waist was shown off by a small, delicately embroidered apron and satin shoes peeped out from her wide skirt. She doubtless told herself it was for the customers' benefit, while knowing that she was really dressing for Richard and the pending interview that she anticipated. She took more than usual care with her hair, and finished with a spray of pomander. As she descended the stairs she steadfastly looked ahead of her, head held high, without glancing into the front bar where she knew Richard would be at work. To catch his eye would unnerve her.

At last Richard appeared and coughed awkwardly. Haltingly, he asked for a private room and there he laid out his heart.

'Be gone with you.' Kit waved her arm in front of her, putting on a severe air that nevertheless he would be able to see was counterfeit; she told him to mind the business of the house as he ought to.

'That will cure you of your pretended passion, which comes about by idleness.'

Richard caught at the words 'pretended' and 'idleness'.

'My dear mistress,' he said, 'if your modesty would allow you to view yourself with the same impartiality as others look upon you, your glass would convince you that nobody is more capable to give love, and consequently mine is not pretended or the effect of idleness . . . No, I love you sincerely; and it is the effect of your agreeable temper. If I have not sooner told you this it was my fear of displeasing you, and losing my place; for I find so great a pleasure in being near, and seeing you, that I prefer that alone to all the profit, were it ten times as much, of your service; and will rather continue your servant, than accept of being master of the best-accustomed house in Dublin, to lose the satisfaction which I find in the sight of you.'

Kit still made herself sound scornful. 'Very romantic truly. No doubt you have been studying some book of compliments, and come to practise upon me.'

'There needs no study to speak the sentiments of my heart,' Richard replied.

'Away to your business.' Kit was keeping up her pretence. 'I don't love flattery; and I know too well the character of your sex to believe a word any one of you utter. I will hear no more. Be gone, I say, and think you are well off that I don't show more anger, which I'm only prevented from doing by your former diligence.'

'You can't be more severe in your punishment of my faults than to banish me thus without the least glimpse of hopes,' said Richard.

'Go, go, repent this impertinence,' she replied. And then at last the glimmer he longed for. 'If you can find a plausible excuse I will give you a hearing tonight when the company has gone.'

Richard seized the moment. 'Oh, let me thank you for this goodness.'

He took her in his arms and almost stifled her with kisses. Although filled with happiness, Kit pretended to be furious, and threatened, if ever he was presumptuous again, she would make him repent it.

'Faith, my dear mistress, you have given me such a taste of happiness that I will undergo any punishment to repeat it.' He at once kissed her again leaving Kit even better pleased, and feigning even more anger.

'Get out of my sight! Go and attend to the customers.'

Richard did as he was bid and Kit stayed behind, composing herself. When she returned to the bar she saw Richard watching her; their eyes met and he could see her blushing when their eyes met. She turned her head away.

He took that as a good omen and when the customers had gone, he went up to Kit's chamber, telling the maid he was going to settle some accounts with her. In a manner of speaking he was.

'How dare you come into my sight!'

'Mistress, as your servant I have always obeyed your orders — and you ordered me to excuse myself for a fault which I own I can't repent.'

He was becoming bolder. 'Indeed, my dear mistress, till you are less inviting I am of the opinion that I shall never be cured of my impertinence, though you may, if you please, change that word and call it as it really is, a sincere, disinterested fondness, by making your man your husband.'

Did he fall on one knee as he continued, 'I will still be your servant. Your happiness and your ease shall be my constant care, and you shall continue as much mistress of what you have, and dispose of it as you now do: for I shall never know any pleasure but that of pleasing you.'

This was doubtless music to Kit's ears — but she told him she was afraid the world would censure her for marrying a servant, a man without a fortune.

His reply was wise. 'Our happiness does not depend on the opinion of the world; for do what we will, we cannot please everybody . . . a great many rich people are strangers to ease and content which they have reason to envy in many of those much beneath them in fortune.

'I will prove the sincerity of my love by keeping you mistress of everything.'

He threw himself on his knees and grasped Kit's in ecstasy. 'Believe me, my dear mistress, I love you for yourself, not for your money, of which I will never pretend to be other than a just steward should you consent to make me the happiest man alive.'

'Get up, it's late, leave me to go to bed.' Kit still hid her true feelings. On the one hand, she was relieved that he was not throwing her onto the bed as Thomas Howell had done — and on the other, she was longing for him to do just that. Instead, she told him she would consider his proposal.

'Let me have one kiss, that I may flatter myself I have recovered your favour, and you shall see me all obedience.'

Kit sighed. 'Well, well, anything to get rid of you.'

At this Richard snatched her in his arms and kissed and embraced her with an ardour that almost took away her senses, and her breath. He left the room, but Kit remained in 'such an agitation, and I fetched my breath so short and thick, that when I had a little recovered myself, I trembled at the risk I had run.' It increased her respect for him, for she knew that had he persisted she would have succumbed.

She realised that with her desire so heightened she could not let him near her chamber again 'until he had a right to do what he pleased, and it would be my duty not to resist him'.

★ ★ ★

Her brief attempt at pretence was over. Just one week later the couple were married. Kit does not record the celebrations, but it is likely to have included much gaiety, for we know Kit had many friends, as well as more customers than any other hostelry in the city.

The church bells would have rung out, and either side of the road from the inn to the church would have been lined with well-wishers. The couple returned to a banquet prepared for them at short notice over the last few frantic days.

The customers had doubtless hung out the bunting, gay flags that had been dyed bright red in cochineal, waving in the breeze outside and hanging from the beams inside. The tables were groaning with food interspersed with pretty displays of posies. The centrepiece may have been a magnificent saddle of venison surrounded by four roast geese and around them a number of roast ducks, together looking like the concentric rings made by a stone dropped in water. Perhaps dribbles of red wine were piped into the venison with minia- ture arrows which, when removed, made the meat run as if with blood.

In the courtyard the dancers rang bells and danced, between downing pints of porter, and all the time a fiddler played, while in a more serene corner the harpist plucked his single row of 41 strings with a quill.

No doubt Kit danced with everyone in turn, stepping out in time and twirling around, but she only had to catch sight of Richard dancing, no matter with whom, for her face to light up, and when they were partnered together she was radiant.

The revelling carried on until, with much cheering, ribaldry and good-tempered banter, the happy couple were piped upstairs to the beribboned four-poster bedstead, its colour- ful cotton and linen twill drapes embroidered with worsted wool in a variety of colourful stitches, and covered in fresh, sweet-smelling flowers.

It all seemed a long time since the Jacobite troubles, and the loss of Kit's father and their land and possessions.

Part II

6

The Fickle Goddess

Kit, pregnant with her third child, reflected once more on her luck. How blissful life was. If ever there was a good man — and she had met those who were not — it was Richard. He had been as good as his promise and still loved and cherished her in every meaning of those words. He was a model husband and he had let her keep her personal effects, so that worry was banished. And her friends, far from censoring her for marrying a servant, complimented her on her choice.

She recorded:

Richard proved a tender, careful and obliging husband; and as he promised, left me as much mistress of my effects as I was when single. Whatever I did was well done, and he never seemed so well pleased, as when he had an opportunity to please me. He neither altered his dress, nor his manner of life; while he was servant he was always tight and clean, which, by the vails [tips] he got, besides his wages, he might very well be. When he was master, he bought neither more suits, nor finer cloth; his change of fortune, made no change in his temper or behaviour; he was altogether as fearful of giving me the least cause of complaint; was humble to our customers, and, if possible, more active and vigilant in our business. He never forgot himself; and if sometimes gentlemen made him sit down with them, he paid them the same deference, and did not saucily, like too many publicans, imagine their conde-scension set him upon a foot with them, and gave him a licence to talk and behave impertinently.

He was remarkable for his sobriety, which, with his modesty, good sense and entertaining wit, endeared him to the best of company that frequented the house. In a word, he had good sense, which he made a proper use of, and never would drown. We lived happily four years with-out any intervening misfortune; in which time I brought him two fine boys and was big with my third child, when the fickle goddess, weary of lavishing on me her favours, turned her back upon me, and resolved to make me sensible that she deserved the epithet of variable.

★ ★ ★

One day Richard left with £50 to pay Alderman Forest in James Street, who supplied their tavern with beer. He did not return, and by the time darkness fell Kit's surprise at his absence turned to anxiety. Fearing he had been murdered for the money he was carrying, she organised a search party. Friends and customers alike scoured the area; every fifth householder was supposed to hang a lantern after nightfall, but where they did not the alleyways were pitch dark. Kit's friends peered along the narrow, crowded streets of the Liberties where criminals mingled without being noticed amongst the market stalls and weaving houses; down to the warehouses by the river; they combed the wasteland by the docks and along each bank of the river.

They found the alderman and he had received the money. Richard had not been robbed but, said the alderman, he 'went away with a gentleman'.

Richard had been a devoted husband and father and shown not a semblance of impropriety during their marriage — he was certainly not the sort to desert his wife — but by nightfall there was still no sign of him and Kit concluded he must have been murdered.

Nothing could console her, and all searches proved in vain. Days turned into weeks and then months. Kit remained overcome by grief. Pregnant, she already had two small children to care for, but all she could think of was Richard and so her business, worked at for so long and so hard, became neglected. She entrusted it to a girlfriend, but instead of improving the situation the friend 'took care of her own interest to the prejudice of mine'. In all too fast a time, Kit had virtually run out of money.

Nearly a year had gone since Richard's disappearance, and in this time Kit gave birth to her third son. Time had alleviated Kit's grief a little and she resolved to take over the running of the inn herself once more, but first she dressed herself and the children in mourning.

★   ★   ★

During Kit and Richard's blissful few years together, war had continued to rage on the continent. France's colourful king, Louis XIV, was constantly trying to make inroads into the Netherlands, seizing many garrison towns along the vital River Meuse. William of Orange, not unnaturally concerned about France's territorial ambitions, sent troops from England to assist his native country, as part of the Grand Alliance, in what became known to some as the Nine Years' War.

Recruiting soldiers to serve in the war was often a hit-or-miss affair. Felons on the run, those escaping unwanted marriages, prisoners offered early release in exchange for fighting, murderers spared the gallows, the homeless and the destitute; all were recruited. Some were tricked into being recruited; a new recruit would be given a shilling ('the king's shilling') after being sworn in, but it was common for a prospective soldier to have the shilling slipped onto his person in an underhand manner, which could then be taken as proof that he had joined up. Most of those who enlisted were illiterate, and wanted nothing more than a weekly wage, as well as somewhere to lay their heads at night.

* * *

Kit, having 'given my dear Richard over for dead', had begun to re-establish her business when, to her surprise, she received a letter from him. We can picture her running to her chamber to open it alone, away from others' eyes. She was in for a shock.

'Dear Christian,' he began (Richard's letter was written in his careful script, and he used her given name). 'This is the twelfth letter I have sent you without answer to my former, which would both surprise and very much grieve me, did I not flatter myself that your silence proceeds from the miscarriage of my letters. It is from this opinion that I repeat the account of my sudden and unpremeditated departure, and the reason for my having enlisted for a soldier.'

A soldier! The words on the parchment shocked her.

It was my misfortune, when I went out to pay the alderman the £50 to meet Ensign C—m, who having formerly been my schoolfellow, would accompany me to the alderman's house, from whence we went, at his request, and took a hearty bottle at the tavern, where he paid the reckoning; having got a little too much wine in my head, I was easily persuaded to go on board a vessel that carried recruits, and take a bowl of punch, which I did in the captain's cabin, where being pretty much intoxicated, I was not sensible of what was doing upon the deck.

Kit must have exclaimed, 'But Richard! You never got drunk, not once, oh, fie.'

Probably the tears began to flow as she read his heart-rending account.

In the interim, the wind sprang up fair, the captain set sail with what recruits were on board, and we had so quick a passage that we reached Helvoet Slys before I had recovered from the effects of liquor.

It is impossible for me to paint the despair I was in, finding myself thus divided from my dear wife and children, landed on a strange shore, without money or friends to support me. I raved, tore my hair and cursed my drunken folly, which had brought upon me this terrible misfortune, which I thought in vain to remedy by getting a ship to carry me back, but there was none to be found.

Kit doubtless subconsciously copied him, tearing at her hair and banging her head on the pillow. She forced herself back to the letter.

The ensign, who possibly did not intend me this injury, did all he could to comfort me, and advised me to make a virtue of necessity, and take on in some regiment. My being destitute and unknown compelled me to follow his advice, though with the greatest reluctance, and I now am, though much against my inclination, a private sentinel in Lord O—'s regiment of foot, where I fear I must pass the remainder of a wretched life under the deepest affliction for my being deprived of the comfort I enjoyed while blessed with you and my dear babies: if providence, in its mercy, does not relieve me; the hopes of which, and of once embracing those alone who engross my tenderest affection, you, my dearest Christian, and my poor children, make me endeavour to support my misfortune, and preserve a life which, without you, would be too miserable to be worth the care of your unfortunate, but ever loving husband, Richard Welsh.

Stupefied and stuffing the letter down her bosom, Kit shrieked and then swooned, falling down apparently lifeless. Friends, or maybe customers, heard the scream followed by the thud and ran to her. No sooner had she come round than she began crying again.

'What's the matter, what is it?' Her friends and neighbours were mystified.

'Richard, my dear Richard, oh must I never see thee more! Oh my dear, dear husband!'

She was in floods of tears. 'Once the comfort of my life, now the source of my misfortunes, I can never support the loss.'

Kit remained in agonies. She felt that although she had bewailed him dead, she found lamenting him while he lived was worse, deprived as he was of any means of returning to her. To Kit the situation was worse than death, for she despaired of his officers letting him go. For days she kept fainting, until her friends feared she was suicidal. They did not know what was wrong with her and she would not tell them but they rallied round her. Had they not taken turns at watching over her at night she admits she would have ended her life.

It was when they were helping her to bed one night that Richard's letter fell from inside her gown. Of course, they read the contents and, at last understanding her trouble, they tried to console her but to no avail.

It was so unlike the Kit of her childhood whose determination and impetuosity were two of her greatest characteristics. When her mother was in danger Kit had thought nothing of risking herself to save her. And there was no braver woman astride a horse.

It was lying in bed one morning, following yet another sleepless night, that Kit's steely resolve finally rose once more; suddenly she knew what to do. Her eyes were illuminated and she lay back on the pillows with a smile that verged on serenity as the idea floated over her, and wrapped itself around her, taking hold, and she fell into the best sleep she had had for days.

In the cool light of dawn she was just as determined. If Richard could not get home to her, she would to go to him.

There were always a number of female camp followers, some who cooked, others who washed, more who whored. But Kit had bolder aspirations, and the thought of going after him eased her 'tortured mind'. She 'flattered herself' that she would find him easily, buy him out of the army, and bring him home to their blissful family life. To most of her friends, she said she was going to England to fetch him home; perhaps she confided her true plan to Mary.

'It's no life for a woman as a camp follower,' Mary probably suggested gently later in the day, glad though she was to see her friend animated at last, 'and how will you begin to know how to find him? It's impossible.'

'Nothing's impossible.'

'Well, then, foolish. And anyway, what about your children, and the business . . . forget it.'

'Forget it? Forget my Richard? Never! And anyway,' Kit added, the idea finally taking clarity, 'who says I'll be a follower?'

She paused, and looked straight into her friend's eyes.

'I'll be a soldier.'

★ ★ ★

Mary knew better than to argue, and Kit at once set about making arrangements; the more she thought of the idea the more possessed she became with it. She would embark with all haste for Flanders, dressed as a soldier to conceal her sex, to search for the man 'whom I preferred to everything else the world could afford me, which, indeed, had nothing alluring in comparison with my dear Richard, and whom the hopes of seeing had lessened every danger to which I was going to expose myself.'

Having the goal helped her regain her strength; the thought of bringing Richard home made her gayer at last, and gave her greater pleasure than at any time during her supposed widowhood. Having made her mind up Kit wasted no time. She arranged for her goods to be left with friends who had room for them, she let the inn to a cooper, and disposed of her children thus: 'my eldest with my mother, and that which was born after my husband's departure, with a nurse, (my second son was dead),

I told my friends, that I would go to England in search of my husband, and return with all expedition after I had found him.'

So, dismissed inside brackets, she told readers that her middle son had died: we do not know how or when (other than at some time since Richard's disappearance); it does seem unsentimental in the extreme, even allowing for the high infant mortality of the time.

Kit arranged for a nurse for the baby, or a wet nurse if she was still breastfeeding. There were always a few available from the homes of upper-class ladies for whom it was considered beneath their dignity to breastfeed, or those paid for by rich ladies' lovers so that the bastard infants could be secreted away and the real mother carry on her social whirl as if nothing had happened. Kit's identity would probably have remained unknown to the wet nurse, but that was not unusual.

She and Richard were of similar size, and she picked out a suit of his clothes; she fitted neatly into his coat and breeches. Her ensemble would have been completed by stockings with frills at the knee, and a white shirt with wide, frilled cuffs that would have peeked out below the turned-back coat sleeves, and a brocaded waistcoat. She quilted this on the inside 'to preserve my breasts from hurt, which were not large enough to betray me'. She probably finished off the ensemble with a fine lace cravat and eyed herself in the looking-glass. The effect was astounding. But Kit was not satisfied. Suddenly she realised what was wrong.

'My hair!' she exclaimed. She grabbed some scissors and cut her hair to just below her ears and level all the way round, as was the custom of common soldiers at the time. Finally she went out and bought some shirts, a hat and wig, and a silver-hilted sword. A further problem remained: money. She would need a lot to buy Richard out of the army and pay for the voyage home; the more money she had, the sooner she was likely to get herself and her husband back home. She solved the dilemma by sewing 50 guineas into the waistband of her breeches.

With a buoyant, free spirit that she had not really felt since growing up on the farm she set off, knowing that if she had to fight like a man to find Richard she would; but deep down she was confident of bringing him home soon.

She made her way briskly towards the docks, walking to the recruitment centre at an inn called The Golden Last. A captain's flag flew alongside its sign and below it a drummer beat in rhythm to the voices of a sergeant and some troopers hailing passing men, urging them to join up.

'Now, gentlemen, think of the gold! There will be booty for all! Imagine the women! Yours for the taking, gentlemen — and the discarding; no more nagging, only entertainment when you want it. And the weapons, gentlemen, the legal weapons . . . Come now, here's five shillings. A crown for you, sir — and canvas over your head.'

He hauled another one in, and another. Kit joined the growing queue without waiting to be encouraged.

★ ★ ★

Kit faced Ensign Herbert Lawrence, the recruiting officer, probably clenching her fingers in fear of being found out. Ensign Lawrence, for his part, must have been surprised to find a zealot ready to fight for the cause rather than someone down on his luck and so any inspection of the 'clever, brisk young fellow' was likely to have been cursory, much to Kit's relief.

Ensign Lawrence swore her in, which meant Kit swore her allegiance to her father's erstwhile enemy, King William. The ensign gave her a guinea as her pay for enlisting, along with a crown with which to drink the king's health.

'You will sail on the next ship, and you will be joining Tichbourne's company of foot in the regiment commanded by the Marquis de Pifare. Lieutenant Robert Gardiner is the company lieutenant. When you reach your regiment in Holland you will be given your arms and uniform and told about your pay. Next!'

For Private 'Christopher' — Kit — Welsh, in search of his missing 'brother', there was now no turning back.

★ ★ ★

To survive the journey across the North Sea, let alone preserve the secret of her sex so early in her mission, was an achievement in itself. The troopships were cramped and crowded and basic in the extreme, with the exception of the captain's quarters. Mortality aboard them was high; pox and plague were rife, along with consumption, scurvy, fluxes and fevers. No wonder they were sometimes described as floating slaughterhouses, with 'the pox above board, the plague within decks, hell in the forecastle and the devil at the helm'. Wastage of men — and horses — was appalling; the horses travelled in the hold, where they could lock their joints to sleep standing up.

The recruits' living quarters were just

above the hold, where their hammocks were slung in rows at night, barely shoulder-width apart. By day, they were folded and stowed away, leaving room for the mess tables to be brought out, where the cramped men ate, drank and played cards. If anything infectious or contagious was going around — and it usually was — it would spread rapidly. The decks above often leaked and so it was hard to keep dry on the voyage. Life was bad enough for those in the midshipmen's quarters; for the men below it was a hellhole.

Had the men washed and changed at night, it would hardly have been possible for Kit to conceal her sex. But they didn't; they slept in their clothes, which made Kit's secret relatively safe. At quiet moments she could visit the heads or seats of ease to relieve herself in comparative privacy. Six heads served 100 men, high up in the bows, their holes lying directly above the sea — if the wind was in the right direction.

The standard of food did little to help their health and to drink water would have been asking for trouble; instead, beer and wine were drunk for as long as supplies lasted. If delayed at sea, or for any reason the ship had been unable to restock supplies while in port, then the beer was likely to be rancid and the salt meat condemned. The staple diet was biscuits, but even these were usually stale and the recruits had to compete with resident weevils consuming the biscuits from within.

Several men would die even on fairly short journeys, whether from the living conditions or even accidents on board the ships. They were given a Christian burial at sea, being wrapped in their hammocks along with some ballast placed at their feet, and then they were slid over the side to the accompaniment of some religious prayers said by the captain, or a clergyman if there was one on board.

The captain was the one person who travelled in relative comfort. His quarters comprised a suite of three sumptuous rooms, a day cabin, a dining room and a sleeping cabin, all finely furnished. The day cabin would contain a leather-bound desk; the dining room would house a long-leaved table surrounded by a dozen or more leather-backed chairs ready for conferences or feasts, when it would be laid with cut glass and silver and china (in contrast to the men's wooden plates and pewter mugs); and the night cabin would feature a luxuriously draped swinging cot, a type of glorified hammock.

The journey from Dublin to Williamstadt in the Netherlands could be expected to take around four days, granted a fair wind and good sailing conditions. Kit's first sight of land would have been a narrow spit to starboard, looming out of an early morning mist, swans emerging from an inlet, and gulls dotted above the otherwise flat horizon. A weak sun shone on the calm water, sheltered by the spit, leaving a strangely yellow reflection. The wide, fiat scrubland to port offered little more of interest, other than that the natural harbour brings a welcome respite from the buffetings of the North Sea. South of today's major Europort near Rotterdam, there are now two road bridges across the inlet that Kit sailed up and from where she and her fellow recruits had their first sight of Williamstadt, encompassed by its star-shaped fortifications. Standing out conspicuously from among the mellow brick and white-painted houses were its domed, octagonal Protestant church and the big town house with its tall clock tower topped by a weather vane of a golden cockerel.

Kit must have looked at the sight with rising excitement and stirring emotion. The first part of her journey was accomplished. Now the real moment of her mission had come.

She must find Richard.

7

A Soldier's Life

Williamstadt was but a brief billet for Kit and her fellow recruits. She had disembarked with a spring in her step and hope in her heart — and doubtless relief at being off that confounded ship. She would find Richard, and soon, of that she was certain. Did she and her fellows have time to explore the small town contained within two rows of star-shaped fortifications and ramparts with a deep strip of water between them, which made the little town almost impregnable? If so, they would have found several alehouses each side of the straight main street. Kit, with her background, already knew much about beer, a mainstay of army life — as were prostitutes, as we shall see.

The next morning, Kit and her fellow men found themselves marching for Gorkumy. There, they were taken by their adjutant to the hospital for examination — again, it was somewhat cursory — and it was self-evident that Kit was able-bodied and free of the pox. She was fit enough to fight, and that was all that mattered.

Kit and the other recruits were issued with their regimentals (uniforms), and first mountings: Holland shirts, blue leggings, and gold-buttoned red tunics topped by the ubiquitous grey coats that were produced in more numbers than any other colour because it was the cheapest. For the officers it came in reasonable quality cloth, but the flimsy material for the men was known as 'sleazy'. The men were given black tricorne hats, except for the grenadiers who had tall, beehive-shaped caps which would not get caught by their arm movement as they threw their grenades; the tricornes soon lost their shape, unlike the better-quality officers' ones where the three sides remained upright. The uniform was finished off with leather shoes with long tongues and big buckles. The mountings included a buff-coloured belt with a frog for the sword worn around the waist, either over or under the coat, a pair of thick gloves and a hide or canvas knapsack in which to carry belongings slung over one shoulder. Kit, slim and work-fit in spite of having borne three children, must have cut a dashing figure. It was to be well into the nineteenth century before routine physical examinations became the norm (at least in the Royal Navy), followed by regulations requiring men to bathe and change their underclothes regularly, and it was probably the same for the army, too.

Once kitted out the recruits were paraded before their commanding officer for his approval, and the next day they found themselves marching again, this time to join the main body of the army at Gertruydenberg. Kit glanced around at the flat land dissected by rows of poplar and willow-lined dykes as she marched along the causeways. It seemed featureless, save for scattered windmills and a few woods, and contrasted greatly with her native Ireland. But she had other things on her mind now. Already she was certain to be enquiring the whereabouts of her 'brother', Richard Welsh.

And always with an eye to the main chance, she was keen to discover how much money she might be paid. She learnt that sentinels like herself in a company of foot were paid 8d per day, of which 6d (2½ pence in today's currency) went on subsistence. There were two paydays per week, when the men were required to put their share into the mess.

They were expected to buy their own food and, when in winter quarters, to pay for their own lodgings. Their clothing was paid for by their colonel, or at least was supposed to be; some were less diligent than others, and the cost of the uniform could easily consume a large chunk of a soldier's wages. On the other hand, they were allowed a ration of gin or rum prior to battle.

Battle! Sure, but she would find Richard before it came to that.

It did not take Kit long to realise that the sutlers — those who sold liquor or provisions to soldiers in camp or garrison — could make a fair living, but only if they, too, abided by strict rules. Each regiment had a grand sutler, (who alone was allowed to the front of the camp) and each troop had a petty sutler.

It was the job of the major to see that the sutler sold no unwholesome provisions or liquor, and to check that the weights and measures they used were correct. Any green fruit was to be destroyed, and any bad bread was to be complained about on delivery, not later. Sutlers who either refused to change the men's money, or obliged them to drink in order to get their money changed, or who demanded a reward for changing money, were liable to be 'plundered and turned out of camp'.

The sutlers kept a few chickens cooped up behind their tents at the rear where larger enclosures contained livestock, mostly cattle but one or two sheep as well. After dark the sutlers' tents were the hive of nightlife in the camp, much like a makeshift inn. It was the picquet captain's nightly duty to put out all the lights in sutlers' tents and to allow no noise to disturb anyone (the picquet was a small outpost, patrol or body of men set apart for some special duty).

Not that there was much noise going on right now, for Kit found herself deployed in a dejected, lacklustre army. It was misty, wet and muddy. A listlessness hung over the vast encampment and demoralisation was written across the faces of men peering from the endless rows of tents with their lines of washing hung between them, strung along the vast, flat plain as they set forth on their daily chores. How on earth was she going to find Richard amongst this interminable panorama?

Not that there was much sign of a battle, their very reason for being here. For months the army had been like this, moving from one siege to another, with all too little to show for it.

★ ★ ★

Kit embroiled herself in her new way of life and relished the challenge posed by concealing her sex. Her competitive spirit and natural abilities soon saw her being noticed by her superiors.

A soldier's day was so full that Kit would have found little time to think of Richard, and even less to look for him. So far every day was the same. Reveille was sounded at 6 a.m.; the soldiers would be on the march before dawn. Water was collected in buckets from the dyke the previous night, when the men were escorted by a corporal of horse or sergeant of dragoons. Cursory washing finished — most men never washed at all — the buckets were then used for calls of nature. Kit must also have somehow concealed and then thrown away her monthly menstrual rags. She would have become adept at scrubbing sweat and fleas off her body with handfuls of straw.

In the period between 1600 and 1770 occasional washing was coming into use; pigs' hair could be used as a rub-down to dislodge lice, and yearly washing of the head in warm water and sweet herbs was followed by cold spring water and found to be refreshing. Cold baths gradually came into vogue, but not to slough away dirt and dead skin cells, rather to give a shock to the system to bring it back into working order. A proverb came into use: wash your hands often, your feet seldom and your head never. Just occasionally people would take a dip in a pond or river. But mostly, make-up and perfume were used to disguise respectively dirt and body odour.

The soldiers, and Kit, had neither.

Those who were rostered for guard duty had to parade before the captain's quarters at 7 a.m., where they were inspected to see that they were clean and smart. The sergeants then marched them to the regimental parade where they were further examined. The assembly for the mounting of the guard was held at 8 a.m., heralded impressively by the beat of the drum major and all the drummers. This was the time when the guards were relieved.

Breakfast was cold porridge, followed by tent tidying and uniform inspection before prayers at 9 a.m., which were read at the head of each brigade. Divine service was held on Sundays, on which day no exercise or firing was allowed.

For the recruits, the morning was spent drilling, drilling, and more drilling.

Then came the broth, insipid but usually hot. It was probably only when she smelt the good wholesome bread freshly baked in the camp ovens that Kit found time to think of home. The bread and broth were followed by stew in tepid gravy with large spots of foul-smelling fat floating about in it, a repast for which they had the dubious privilege of paying a portion of their pay. But as they would get nothing more until evening, and the afternoon's marching practice would rekindle their appetites, they usually paid for it, if grudgingly.

It was a rule that officers should wear their regimentals whilst in camp. They were also responsible for ensuring their men were well dressed with their shirts tucked in and wearing marching gaiters, as well as possessing 24 rounds of ammunition each.

Twice a week captains inspected the men's clothes, while it was the duty of the subalterns to check them every morning before the men left camp. The rule that tents had to be opened and aired every morning before being checked by officers came naturally to Kit, but she was only allowed to collect water once or twice a day.

Army life meant more than concealing her sex, for Kit had been her own master for a number of years and was a businesswoman of renowned aptitude. But now she discovered rules that would curtail her natural instincts, on penalty of death. There were usually two men to a tent and Kit is likely to have been the better educated. Perhaps she read out some of the rulebook to her companion (for the illiterate, the rules were drummed into them by those who could read).

'Listen to this, it's the death penalty if we kill game, or go hunting or fowling or even for shooting in camp.' She fingered her musket and exclaimed, 'Or anyone caught fishing, pond-draining or dyke-cutting, or selling forage. And,' she paused, 'any soldier who takes his arms out of the bell tent after retreat at 7 p.m. also faces the firing squad. Oh, and we can't sell powder, ball or ammunition either, unless we want severe punishment.'

The most usual offence was desertion, for which the sentence was to be severely flogged or even shot at the head of the offender's regiment.

Kit read on. 'It says trivial or light offences will be punished by confinement, drill or extra duty, so severe punishment must be more than that. And no one is allowed to inscribe arms with their own initials or mark.'

Their major went on his rounds checking all candles were snuffed. Kit just had time to read that courts martial were only to be held for crimes considered so bad that they merited public whipping, and with that floating in her head she snuffed the candle and turned in; her tent-mate was probably already snoring.

★　★　★

There was more to learn, but for now it was a period of intensive training for Kit and her fellow recruits. Kit continued to excel, and was not at all modest when reminding readers, 'I was accustomed to soldiers as a girl when I loved to see them exercise, and I was soon perfect and applauded by my officers for my dexterity.'

We can imagine the scene.

'Charge your bayonets breast high.'

Kit was nimble and proficient at the task so that while the other recruits were still fumbling with their unfamiliar weapons, she already had hers in the right position. It was what she had dreamed of all those years ago when James II had been proclaimed King; now there was nothing imaginary about what she was doing.

'How you lot think you'll beat the French, God only knows,' the sergeant bellowed again. 'Who are we going to beat?'

'The enemy, sir,' one recruit piped up.

'And who's the enemy?'

'The French, sir.'

'And how are we going to do that, pray? None of you can even aim straight. Right. Start again. Charge your bayonets breast high; come briskly to your recover; briskly, I said, briskly. For God's sake, why are we doing this?'

'For the king, sir.'

'No, no, no, no. No, because the French

94

want to overrun all of us, that's why, they're trying to take control of all of us, make us slaves and rule all of Europe. God preserve us. Imagine that, all of Europe under the tyrant of France.' He shuddered exaggeratedly.

'So, come on. Drill. Quit your right hand — no, you over there, your right hand — and bring it under the butt of your piece. God, you're a useless lot. Welsh, come up here and show them how it's done.'

Kit stepped forward, and demonstrated as he issued directions.

'Face full to the right. Charge by placing your piece against your breast, over the bend of your left arm — as with a pike.

'Now, push your bayonet, push it directly outright.'

He glanced at Kit and continued. 'Bring it again to your breast. Recover your firelocks. Quit your right hand from the butt and seize behind the lock. Recover.'

The men tried again and showed a slight improvement, and he dismissed them.

8

I Heard the Cannon Play

It was back to more exercise for two hours every afternoon in addition to their morning drilling in the recruits' packed day. When would Kit ever find a chance to look for Richard? But, for now, her attention would be taken up by the modern weaponry to which the men were adapting. The matchlock musket had been slow and cumbersome, and vulnerable to damp. Between shots, the musketeer was defenceless against cavalry, unless protected by pikemen. So a bayonet was added on to the musket, but once the bayonet was put into its fixed position, the musket could no longer be fired. The army was to wait a few more years yet until in 1697 the socket bayonet was introduced, easing the fixing and unfixing by having a rigid lock on the musket. The flintlock musket had a snapcock which showered sparks onto gunpowder when the trigger was pulled, and it increased the rate of fire, so that by 1700 a well-trained man could fire a shot a minute. Between 1692 and 1697, during the war that Kit now found herself a part of, bandoliers and powder horns were generally replaced by made-up paper cartridges in pouches that speeded things up even more, so the time of Kit's training was one of great advancement in the military.

There was even more for her to discover about camp life, too. And before long there was to be her first taste of battle.

Kit had read more of the regulations. Each day's orders started by naming the field officers of the day, and by detailing the composition of the different picquets, according to a roster kept by the brigade major; it was his duty to ensure no contingent or regiment was called on for more than its fair share. Next to be rostered were the guards over the quarters of the various officers, and finally any escorts that might be needed during the day were selected. When an officer was on guard, his servant was required to go with him as a duty man.

A surgeon was always present at parades; if a soldier had to go to hospital all of his accoutrements, ammunition, watch coat and other military articles had to be put in the company store chests; recruits were not allowed watch coats. Maybe Kit instinctively drew her blanket around her when she read this.

No soldier was allowed out of camp without leave, and any who passed beyond the outermost guard were deemed deserters. When soldiers wanted to go to market they had to be accompanied by a sergeant who was also answerable for their behaviour. An officer also had to be with them when they went off to cut wood. It was forbidden for young trees or avenues of trees to be cut down.

If there was an outbreak of fire, three cannon shots were fired to summon all men and officers to their colours at a pre-arranged regimental alarm post. She finished reading and let out a little sigh; she had surely never felt more confined or restricted in her life. If Richard's regiment was camped somewhere else she would not be able to look for him at all. Right now she would be unable to search anyway, for the next day they marched to Landen where Kit heard that the enemy was all around and battle was rumoured to be imminent; first, however, she was put on night duty.

She was escorted to her assignment by an officer, skirting some apple and pear trees along the way (the fruit not yet ripe, Kit may have noted), until they arrived at quarters of the Elector of Hanover. Here she was posted at the bedchamber door as part of the night guard.

The electorate of Hanover was the ninth electorate of the Holy Roman Empire; Germany was made up of many principalities at this time, but some of them had the added eminence of being the electors who chose the Holy Roman Emperor, a key figure in the Grand Alliance alongside William. The Elector of Hanover at this time was Ernest Augustus, Duke of Brunswick, whose son was to become King George I of Great Britain and Ireland.

The elector was housed in the village and the first thing Kit would have seen as she entered his chambers was a large table laden with silverware and lit by a chandelier; an elegant pair of candle snuffers lay in their open box on the elegant sideboard and several empty wine flagons were scattered around. Orderlies were clearing them away, along with the remnants of the elector and his friends' nightly repast; judging by the amount of cutlery, there must have been at least five courses.

Later, when the guests and most of the staff had gone, Kit's eyes opened wide at the oncoming visitor. She remained motionless as the duke's valet-de-chambre, a Turk named Mustapha, introduced to him 'a fine, handsome jolly lady, who was what we call a black beauty; she was dressed in rich silk, and her gown was tied with ribbons from her breast to her feet.' She was ushered into the elector's bedchamber where he lay handsomely in bed.

While the antics of the Elector of Hanover may have made Kit smile, her next assignment did not: she was still on night duty and yet to be relieved when the Battle of Landen began. For the first and the last time in her account, she admits to being afraid as she heard the first shots ring out. It was 29 July 1693, and she was 26 years old, but it has to be noted that there is a huge anomaly here: Kit's father died after the Battle of Aughrim in 1691 and it was supposedly *after* this that Kit, by then penniless, was courted and deflowered by Thomas Howell, which led to her going to her aunt's pub in Dublin, serving her for four years before being left the pub, marrying Richard Welsh and having a number of children. Yet here we are, two years after Aughrim, at Landen in 1693!

Of Landen, Kit wrote, 'I heard the cannon play, and the small shot rattle about me, which, at first, threw me into a sort of panic having not been used to such rough music.

'However, I recovered from my fear.'

Her apprehension was not groundless, for as Kit was returning early in the morning to report back to her regiment, she was grazed by a musket ball in her ankle.

'I was carried from the field at Lord Cholmondley's orders and was out of service for two months.'

So Kit dismissed her first taste of battle very simply; and, equally importantly, her success in keeping her sex secret, in spite of hospital treatment. Two months out of action makes one suspect the wound was more than a mere graze, even allowing for the lack of modern medical facilities. However, she says, Lord Cholmondley 'expressed concern for my ankle injury in very humane terms'.

Among those lost fighting for the French was Kit's erstwhile neighbour Patrick Sarsfield, first Earl of Lucan. He had fought in Ireland for the Jacobites including at the Battle of Aughrim where Kit's father was lost, and Sarsfield earned high praise for his conduct after the battle and in brokering the Treaty of Limerick before he sailed to France (with some of the so-called 'Wild Geese'), there to end up fighting William once more.

Landen was a disaster for the Allies and a decisive victory for the French cavalry who at their fourth attempt broke through William's earthwork fortifications, enabling them to capture the village from the rear. William himself led a brave rearguard of English and Scottish troops, which saved the Allied army from annihilation. The Dutch infantry loyally rallied to William after this defeat, ready to rebuild and fight again.

Kit noted that her record of the battle was more impartial than the enemy account 'being too vain', or the English writers who lessened 'too much the loss we there sustained'.

★ ★ ★

By the time Kit was passed fit to resume her duties it was winter time, and she and her fellow comrades were quartered in the fortified city of Gertruydenberg. But the allied soldiers found conditions little better there than in the mud and mist of camp, for although they were billeted in dry houses and were free to go out carousing at night, they were put to arduous work by day, much of it in rebuilding crumbling dykes, which brought its own dangers.

Kit was out among the dykes that had been ruined by worms, drowning a complete village, with Ensign Robert Gardiner, her company lieutenant, one day. They were working in waist-deep water, and as the incoming tide approached, most of the men had already left; but Lieutenant Gardiner and Kit were working away so hard, trying to ensure everything was secured, that they 'narrowly escaped drowning by the tide coming in upon us; however, we supported each other, and waded out hand-in-hand long after the others had gone off'.

A worse mishap was to follow.

9

Courting a Girl and Fighting a Duel

How did Richard feel during the summer of
1694, which was conspicuous for its lack of
military action, and boredom was endemic
among the men? Was he writing more letters
in vain to Kit, believing her still to be in
Dublin? Did he continue to hate a soldier's
life, and to miss his wife and family as much
as he intimated in the letter Kit received? Did
he yearn to be in Dublin and hold her in his
arms again? We can only guess at the answers,
whereas Kit, it appears, was very much
becoming immersed in her new life.

★   ★   ★

Richard would have been more concerned
than ever had he known what had just
befallen Kit. She was among a contingent of
English and Dutch soldiers out foraging
when they were caught unawares by a French
detachment. Before they had time to defend
themselves they were captured, about 60 of
them, and ignominiously stripped of their

uniforms, and 'by very tiresome march' forced to Saint-Germain-en-Laye.

There they lay, semi-naked and huddled together during the long, dark night, little knowing what would become of them; Kit makes no mention of how she concealed her sex. The next day King James's Queen, Mary of Modena, intervened on behalf of the English. They were separated from the Dutch and given straw bedding, and, as Kit related,

the Dutch were given none, and we were allowed five farthings per man per day for tobacco, a whole pound of bread and a pint of wine a day for each man; moreover our clothes were returned to us. The other prisoners had but half a pound of bread a day, drank water, and lay almost naked, in filthy dark prisons, without other support.

The Duke of Berwick [fighting for the French] frequently came to see that we were well used, and not defrauded of our allowance. He advised us to take on in the French service, as seven of the English did. He spoke to me in particular.

I answered, 'I have taken an oath already to King William, and if there is no crime in breaking it, as I am satisfied it is one of the blackest dye, I could not in honour break my engagement. There is nothing in my opinion more unbecoming an honest man and a soldier, than to break even his word once given.

The choice was left to her.

More than a week went by when suddenly the remaining British prisoners heard a trumpet sounding outside; within moments they discovered that Mr Van-Dedan, the trumpeter (who ended up as a Chelsea Pensioner), had come to restore their liberty, their freedom having been exchanged for a number of captive French. The first thing they did was go to the Château de Saint-Germain-en-Laye, which had been provided for James II and Queen Mary by Louis XIV, to thank the Queen for the good work she had done on their behalf. She spoke to them individually and told Kit she was a 'pretty young fellow' and it grieved her that she had not obtained her freedom sooner.

* * *

Soon it was winter once more and Kit was quartered in Gorkham where 'my grief for my husband being drowned in hopes of finding him, I indulged in the natural gaiety of my temper and lived very merrily'.

Not for the first time she had been referred to in high places as a 'pretty fellow'. Perhaps it was time to scotch any tongues that might be wagging and prove her masculinity. Or it may simply have been her childhood love of frolicking again, as well as to kill time in the long, boring winter, that she began making advances to the pretty young daughter of a burgher.

Kit had had many amorous passes made at her as a girl in Leixlip and so she was 'at no loss in the amorous dialect; I ran over all the tender nonsense (which I look upon as a lover's heavy cannon, as it does the greatest harm with raw girls) employed in such attacks . . . I squeezed her hand whenever I could get an opportunity, sighed often in her company; looked foolishly and practised upon her all the ridiculous airs which I had often laughed at, when they were used as snares against myself'.

Kit got more than she bargained for in more ways than one, leading her to repent of her larking, the first being that the girl got fond of her, and chided her if so much as half a day went by without seeing her. The girl went to lengths to get whatever she could for her beau, and declared her passion, saying she loved Kit better than life itself. At the same time she remained virtuous.

Perhaps they were walking hand in hand along the banks of the river, admiring the swans' reflection in the water made different shades of pink by the setting sun, when Kit made a pass at her. The girl's reaction was stinging.

'I suppose my tenderness for you has become irksome,' she said, 'since you seem to be trying to turn it into hatred. If you've got dishonourable designs upon me, you're not the man I love.

'I've been mistaken — you're nothing but a ruffian.

'And to think, I had hoped you might be a tender husband for me.'

Still Kit did not own up. Instead, the girl's rebuff gained her heart. She took the girl in her arms and said, 'You've heightened the power of your charms by your virtue; it would make me love you more were it not that you already engross all my tenderness.'

Kit admits that she had become fond of the girl, but recorded, 'Mine, you know, could not go beyond a platonic love.'

Nevertheless they continued to see each other, and it became well known in the regiment and beyond that Kit and the girl were 'an item', to use a modern idiom. As the girl was a wealthy burgher's daughter, Kit's esteem doubtless also went up in some quarters — though not all . . .

Kit was on duty at her post one day standing to arms when suddenly the girl came up to her, in a dreadfully distressed state and begging Kit to help her.

Kit describes the story through military analogy:

A sergeant of our regiment but not of the company I belonged to, sat down before the citadel of her heart, and made regular approaches, which cost him a number of sighs and a great deal of time; but finding I commanded there, and it was impossible to take by a regular siege, he resolved to give a desperate assault, sword in hand.

One day, therefore, while I was under arms, he came to her, and without any previous indication of his design, a fair opportunity offering, he very bravely, and like a man of honour, employed force to obtain what he could not get by assiduity.

The girl defended herself stoutly, and in the scuffle she lost her cap, and her clothes were most of them torn off her back; but notwithstanding her resolute defence, he had carried the fortress by storm, had not some of the neighbours opportunely come in to her assistance, alarmed by her shrieks, and made him retreat in a very shameful manner.

The poor girl, having poured out her tale to Kit, begged her to help. 'You will revenge his insult, yes?'

The memory of Thomas Howell ravishing Kit would doubtless have risen up in her mind. She was furious and could hardly contain herself; she paled and her whole body shook, but she was on duty and so could do nothing immediately, 'or I should that instant have sought and killed him'.

As soon as she was dismissed she searched out her rival. Striding along the track as if it was the springy peat turf of Ireland, head down, blood boiling, sword swinging at her side, she may not have noticed a young deer as it crossed her path, its big, liquid eyes resembling two dark, round, deep pools as it paused to gaze at her. Its long, spindly legs looked too fragile to propel it over a high paling into a field of young wheat, there to join some of its herd who were already nibbling the sweet green shoots.

It did not take Kit long to track down her quarry and straight away she confronted him.

'How dare you?' she cried. 'How dare you attempt the honour of a woman who for all you know could be my wife? You know very well that I have long been making honourable love. Your action was so base that you're not worthy of wearing the king's cloth, and you cast a poor reflection on the whole corps.'

'You're nothing but a proud, prodigal coxcombe,' the sergeant retorted scornfully.

'I leave Billingsgate language to women and cowards,' Kit declared. 'I haven't come here for a tongue battle but to exact reparation of honour.'

She pointed towards a windmill.

'If,' her blood was up, 'you have as much courage in the face of a man as you have in assaulting a defenceless woman, go with me instantly to that windmill yonder.'

★ ★ ★

How far away was Richard at this moment? Perhaps he was resting first on one foot and then the other, cold, stiff and bored while on piquet guard. Did he bang his gloved hands together and whistle silently through clenched teeth? He shouldn't be here. Damn this war. Damn that day in Dublin. Damn . . .

Perhaps he would try writing to Kit again. But what was the point? He had not heard from her. He might as well give up. Maybe it was time for him to join in with his fellows a bit more, enjoy some of the fun that they did. Whatever he was thinking, he will have returned to his tent once off duty oblivious to the danger his beloved wife was in at that very moment.

* * *

Their swords clashed and their tongues lashed as Kit nimbly danced around her clumsy opponent, and with her first thrust she caught him on his right breast, but it was only a slanting wound that did little damage.

By now mindless of her own danger in issuing such a challenge — for she could be sentenced to death if caught being out of camp without permission and with arms while off duty, never mind the possibility of being killed in a duel — she recorded, 'I was so irritated at the ill-usage of my sweetheart and the affront put on me in person that I thought of nothing but putting this villain out of the world.'

Kit knew the sergeant had risen from a mere footman and his rank had evidently gone to his head. As the fight continued below the windmill passers-by began to gather round. The sergeant lunged at her and she raised her left arm to protect her body; she received a long gash but her sword arm was good and, before he could recover his guard, Kit thrust her sword into his right thigh, inches from his groin — 'about half a span from the pope's eye'.

He doubled over momentarily, then with renewed vigour — and both combatants oblivious to the gathering crowd cheering them on — he aimed his next pass at her chest. Kit was as nimble as a gazelle and it caught her right arm instead. But it was little more than a pinprick, for by now his leg wound was bleeding profusely and he was becoming feeble through loss of blood, forcing him to stagger to the ground.

The sound of galloping hooves came thundering up and a file of passing musketeers on duty with their sergeant drew rein, firing a shot into the air. Kit was standing over her man, legs apart and sword raised. A musketeer grabbed her from behind, forced the sword from her hand and tied her wrists behind her as the sergeant writhed on the ground, moaning.

But for this intervention, Kit would surely have killed the weakened man with her next thrust, would have been executed herself, and there her story would have ended. She was extremely lucky that it did not.

Her gravely injured opponent was stretch-
ered straight to hospital while Kit was taken
to prison as 'both the aggressor and a common
soldier'.

*   *   *

It was cold and dark and cheerless in prison
with little to offer a soldier like Kit. It would
have been small and quite possibly smelly and
damp; she may have had to share a bundle of
straw to sleep on with resident rats and had a
bucket in one corner to serve as a toilet. But
quite probably nothing would depress Kit at
this point, for she had revenged the insult to
her maiden. She managed to obtain writing
materials, for she wrote to the girl and told
her what had happened and that she was now
in prison.

She must have begun to fear she would
moulder there indefinitely — or at least until
sentenced to death — when, on the fourth
day, she was surprised to hear the cell door
open, and to be told she was free. Her sword
was returned, her arrears of pay given, and
she was also discharged from her regiment.

The girl, on receipt of Kit's letter, had told
her father, the burgher, what had happened,
and it was he who had procured the pardon
from King William himself.

The moment she was free Kit hastened to thank the girl. She got more than she bargained for, though. The girl not only thanked Kit for risking her life for her. She also proposed that they get married.

10

Becoming a Dragoon — and a 'Father'

Kit thought quickly, her mind racing.

'My dear,' she said, 'you offer me the greatest happiness this world can afford me. I'll ask your father.'

'My father!' the girl exclaimed, jumping up in alarm, both hands in the air. 'No, no, you can't do that!'

'Why not?' Kit asked, feigning innocence.

'You cannot imagine a rich burgher will give his daughter to a foot soldier,' she said, adding, 'for though I think you merit everything, yet my father will not view you with my eyes.'

She suggested instead that they should elope. She would 'run the hazard of your fortune, in case my father proves irreconcilable after our marriage.'

'My dear life!' Kit exclaimed. 'There are two insuperable obstacles. How could I bear to see you deserted by your father, deprived of a fortune, and stripped of all the comforts of life, exposed to hardships and insults to which women who follow a camp are liable?

'And how can I, with honour, consent to bring your father's grey hairs to the grave in sorrow, by robbing him of a daughter he tenderly loves, by way of return for having procured my liberty?' Kit asked.

'No, my charmer, though I am no more than a common soldier,' — she was warming to her theme — 'this breast is capable of as much tenderness and contains as much honour as that of a general.'

Beating her chest, she continued, 'I cannot be so inhuman to you or unjust to your father. But, as I shall know no satisfaction in life if deprived of you, it will spur me to raise my rank so your father need not be ashamed of our alliance.

'Or else,' she added dramatically, 'I shall put an end to life which must be miserable without you.

'The sword, my dear, ennobles, and I don't despair of a commission as I have some reputation in the army, many friends, and I am not destitute of money.

'I think it more becoming the character of a soldier to gain a commission by bravery than to purchase one with money; but my desire to call you mine will make me endeavour to deserve you, and I will, if possible, purchase a pair of colours.'

At first the girl was not impressed. 'I have

heard,' she said, 'that love and reason are incompatible; this maxim is either false, or you are not the ardent lover you profess yourself. However, I relish your proposal of buying a commission, and if you fall short of money let me know.'

'You call the ardour of my passion in question, because I love you for yourself,' Kit said. 'I wish to make you, if possible, as happy in our union as I shall be; while most other men have their own satisfaction alone in view, when they address the fair sex.

'I accept your offer with a grateful sense of obligation; but hope I need not put you to the proof of your friendship, unless some misfortune should deprive me of what I have saved.'

★ ★ ★

At this time commissions could be purchased. A dead officer's military equipment was sold at the head of his regiment during first parade, when there was also a keen interest in purchasing his rank, usually by the next in line, for a set price; only in times of war, when many men might be killed, could ordinary soldiers have any chance of promotion. It was, however, still possible to earn promotion, and this is what Kit vowed to do.

However, the only mention she ever again gave of her maiden in her account was, 'thus I got off from this *amour* without loss of credit.'

★ ★ ★

Having been discharged from Lord Tichborne's Company of Foot, but not the army, Kit felt disinclined to leave the service altogether, which would mean she would have to break into her capital sum, still sewn, presumably, in her breeches. So she decided she must join another regiment; remaining in her previous company would be untenable, given the animosity that would exist towards her once her duelling foe recovered sufficiently, especially as he was of a higher rank.

How did she come to choose Lord John Hay's regiment of dragoons? Was it the grey horses? Did they rekindle the daredevil riding exploits of her youth? Certainly, her reputation would have gone before her: a highly praised soldier who had fought a duel to defend the honour of 'his' young lady.

Did Kit mention to her fellows that her lover wanted them to marry? Did this raise her reputation even higher or did they simply suppose she had got her pregnant? However it came about, it was to Lord John Hay's

Dragoons, the forerunner of the Royal Scots Greys, that she transferred.

★ ★ ★

One can imagine the scene: Kit standing to attention inside a large, well-appointed tent and saluting smartly.

'At ease.' Lord John Hay was a dapper man who was always to be seen neatly dressed. He expected his men — and their horses — to be turned out equally well.

'Your reputation travels before you, Welsh.'

'Yes, Sir.'

'Well, I want to make one or two things clear. We are here to fight a war against the French, not our officers.' His upper lip gave a twitch and his steely eyes looked straight into hers. 'And we undertake our daily tasks dutifully, which does not include rescuing damsels in distress. I believe my regiment is the best, and I wish it to remain that way. Do I make myself clear?'

'Yes, Sir.'

'Word has reached me that you have an excellent record and I am therefore prepared to overlook duels and affairs but if you so much as step out of line once again, don't expect another chance.'

'No, Sir.'

'We expect to be marching soon, you've heard?'

'I have, Sir. And it's my greatest desire to fight and beat the French.'

'That's the spirit, good man. Welcome to my regiment of dragoons, you are now a trooper. God go with you.'

'Thank you, my lord.'

She was taken in hand by Lieutenant Keith whose quarters she shared.

★ ★ ★

Kit at once found she was in a smart regiment, with far higher morale than she had so far encountered, almost like an island of hope surrounded by the demoralised main army, listlessly awaiting action. This had much to do with the meticulous manner in which Lord Hay went about procuring cloth for uniforms and harness for horses through his agent in Scotland. Lord Hay was the second son of the Marquess of Tweedale, and had received a commission as Captain in the Royal Scots Dragoons in July 1689 before steadily rising up the ranks. Most of his men were Scottish, and pride and camaraderie were evident to Kit all around her.

The Dragoons had arrived in the Low Countries earlier that year, 1694, having been reviewed by William III in Hyde Park before their departure when, for the first time on record, they were all mounted on grey horses. This probably accounted for their subsequent title, within a decade, of Royal Scots Greys, though one school of thought claims the name arose from the ubiquitous grey cloth of their uniforms; however, as this was worn by most soldiers of all regiments in the late seventeenth century, the grey horses is probably the right answer.

The grey coats were replaced by red coats with blue facings, proclaiming their royal status. After this first review when the regiment was mounted on all-grey horses it became increasingly known as the Grey Dragoons or the Scots Regiment of Grey Dragoons, the Royal Scots Greys, or simply the Scots Greys.

Kit now had new drilling and tactics to learn as a dragoon and once more she excelled. She was also kept under much closer surveillance by her superiors than before, althought that did not stop her getting up to mischief again.

Being billeted with an officer, however, gained her access to up-to-date information, and Lieutenant Keith is likely to have explained her new role as a dragoon to her.

'Dragoons are a cross between cavalry and

infantry,' he will have told her. 'We ride horses but in battle we are just as likely to be called upon to dismount and fight on foot.'

'What happens to the horses?'

'One man in every ten stays behind to hold them.'

Kit probably listened with her chin cupped in her hand as they sat in their shared tent, bigger than she was accustomed to on account of Keith being a junior officer.

'We're often used for reconnaissance or manning outposts, or as escorts and many other jobs, often clearing the way in advance of the cavalry — they are the smartest of all — so you see why we're often called the handymen of the Army.'

'Sounds much more interesting than being a foot soldier,' Kit said. In truth, it was a role that could have been made for her. She was probably disappointed to learn they were not allowed to gallop their horses, though.

She tried on her new uniform with its smart red frock coat, and boots, which were of lighter, suppler leather than those of the cavalry, to enable dragoons to walk as well as ride. Then she fingered her new weaponry, casting her eye up and down the carbine.

'The musket's shorter than I had in the Foot,' she observed.

'You'll find it easier to handle when you're

riding,' Keith said, also giving her a bayonet, hatchet and straight sword, all of which Kit would now have to become adept at using. It did not take her long.

'You'll find our Major a good man, too, George Preston. I'd say he won't be long in leaping up to Brigadier.'

'Is it true my pay will be better?'

'Yes, although it's less than the Horse, it's more than the Foot; you'll be getting daily pay of one shilling and twopence, plus eight shillings and twopence subsistence, but don't forget you have to pay for the keep of your horse yourself.'

The cavalry (horse) pay was 2/6d (12½ pence) a day, plus 14 shillings a week subsistence.

'Oh, and you're allowed three rounds of ammunition — that's for guarding the horses when they're turned out to grass.'

Kit looked questioningly.

Keith said, 'It's different in battle; the Horse will only have three rounds and mainly use their swords because they're backed up by the Infantry's firepower.'

'And us?'

'We sometimes fight on foot, so we're allowed more rounds.' He noted Kit's interest. 'You'll get the knack of it in training.'

Kit made a fine figure in her uniform and her good looks were noted quite literally from the highest — Lord Hay referred to her as his 'pretty dragoon' — to the lowest, having caught the eye of a particular prostitute.

No sooner had Kit mastered the new weapons and techniques of a dragoon than she was deployed for action in the Siege of Namur, which was led by King William himself.

Namur lies in a valley gorged by the Rivers Meuse and Sambre, with a cliff-like escarpment on one side and a gentler hill on the other. This strategic position made it inevitable that its citadel, high up on the escarpment (which visitors reach today by cable car or steep winding road), was the target of many military attacks, but after the French captured it in 1692 they had strengthened it so significantly that it was considered impregnable.

Now, three years later, and the Allies, in a surprise move by King William, were attempting to win it back by siege. Kit recorded, 'Never was more terrible fire seen; no less than sixty large battering pieces and as many mortars played incessantly on the outworks, which rose one above another in the form of an amphitheatre.'

Most of the fortifications were demolished and breaches made that were large enough for a battalion to mount in front; eventually, an assault was ordered after the batteries had played with greater fury than ever.

'My Lord Cutts with 3,000 English was commanded to assault the new castle,' Kit wrote, 'and when the signal was given those troops marched with incredible intrepidity. Here our brave English were drawn into a fatal mistake by their courage, for 300 of them mounted the breach of the new castle with such impetuosity that they could not be supported; by this ardour we failed in the attack of that work. The other assault proved more successful. We carried all the covered way of the Devil's House and that of Fort Koehoorn. Here we made our lodgements, which being joined, we were masters of 3,000 yards of covered way.'

Baron John Cutts, colonel of the Coldstream Guards, was considered witty, vain and conceited, and was remembered as both brave and brainless for his reckless courage at Namur, where he earned the nickname Salamander, by which he is still remembered.

★ ★ ★

Winter quarters were in Boss, and as usual much time was spent in houses of civil recreation.

One night Kit walked into such an establishment with two of her colleagues. One can imagine the scene: they ordered some ale and made their way through the crowd to a small table. On it were a pack of cards and some dice, but of more interest to Kit's two colleagues were two heavily powdered women sporting curly blonde locks. The women leant so far across them at the table that their breasts appeared in danger of leaving their low-cut supports. Tight bodices ensured slim waists which the women swung sexily first this way, and then that, pouting their red-painted lips as they did so. The two soldiers lost no time in 'making a bargain for and retiring with such ware as they wanted', and so Kit moved over to a corner and settled down to serenading the remaining company by playing the tongs and key, an instrument used for burlesque music, entertaining them with joke tunes that caricatured serious music.

While there, a very large prostitute took a liking to her 'for I made a better figure than any other dragoon' — modesty was never a strong point of Kit's — and the lady 'used all the common methods of those virtuous damsels to entice me'.

Unsurprisingly no amount of proposition-ing would lure Kit and so, slighted by the rebuttal, the lady swore she would seek revenge.

She did just that, some while later, by 'swearing me the father of her child. Whether this was the effect of her revenge, or her judgement, as I made a better figure than any private dragoon in our regiment, and she thought me the best able to provide for her in her month, and to take care of her bastard, is what I won't take upon me to determine; I was so surprised and enraged at the impudent perjury that I was almost tempted to disprove her effectually.'

But her love of soldiering won over and she paid up. However, the child lived only one month.

And, once more, Kit had heightened her reputation among her peers.

11

Corporal John

Kit's life as a soldier could well have ended with the Treaty of Ryswick, signed on 20 September 1697; it brought to an end the tedious and inconclusive Nine Years' War. With the Dutch generals having showed no desire to entice the enemy into battle, there had been little military action for the last two years, so Kit and her fellows had had little chance to show their worth in the field.

Instead, King William reviewed the army at Breda and then disbanded it. Many of the soldiers returning home would not be able to find work; but although Kit had a family and business to return to, she chose not to. She sailed from Brill, another star-shaped fortified port in south Holland, to Dublin all right, but once there, she only glimpsed her family from afar, while remaining incognito.

Why the disguise, the subterfuge? Was it truly that she loved the double life she was leading? Her husband, Richard, had not been mentioned in her text for some while, yet the search for him was her original motive for joining up. Her early account of married life shows she was a good mother and wife, and an excellent businesswoman. Had her youthful tomboy days re-emerged to such an extent as a soldier that she felt truly immersed in that life? Or was it pure parsimony, in not wanting to pay out more money for them?

She states simply that 'on enquiry, I found my mother, children and friends wanted neither health nor the necessaries of life. I found means to converse with them, but I was so much altered by my dress and the fatigues I had undergone that not one of them recognised me, which I was not sorry for.'

The truth is revealed next. 'The demand the nurse had upon me, on account of my youngest child, being greater than my circumstances to discharge, I resolved to remain incognito.'

Yet she had never broken into her capital (the sum of 50 guineas that she had quilted into her waistband when she enlisted), which, she says, she had husbanded with great economy.

After checking on her family, she 'was not long easy in this indolent way of life which must soon have drained my purse, wherefore I sought any employment and found means to support myself.'

We neither hear what work she took nor

how she lived over the next fours years only that, once the battle drums rolled again in 1701, 'Christopher' Welsh was one of the first to sign up, rejoining Lord Hay's Dragoons, along with Lieutenant Keith once more.

★ ★ ★

King William and the mighty French king, Louis XIV, had genuinely tried to avoid further war by agreeing who should succeed to the Spanish throne upon the expected imminent death of the childless Spanish king, known as Charles the Sufferer. The son of Philip IV of Spain, he was the victim of generations of inbreeding, leaving him both mentally and physically retarded.

They agreed on Prince Joseph of Bavaria, but he died a few months later; next they agreed to the Emperor Leopold's son, Archduke Charles, only to be confounded by the dying Spanish king himself, who on his deathbed bequeathed the throne to his 16-year-old grand-nephew, Louis XIV's grandson, Philip, Duke of Anjou.

As Philip was already second in line to the French throne, the prospect — only one step removed — of a joint monarchy between France and Spain and all they owned between them, was unthinkable to the

English and Dutch.

Louis, perhaps unsurprisingly, accepted the will and promptly moved his army forwards into the Spanish Netherlands and took possession of the Dutch-occupied barrier fortresses, so wiping out William's years of patient campaigning at one stroke. To compound tensions further, Louis XIV, on the death in exile of James II in France in 1701, announced that he recognised James's son, also James, and known as the Old Pretender, as rightful king of England, rather than William and Mary, or any of their children.

In fact, William and Mary produced no children (Mary's sister Anne subsequently became Queen). They were first cousins, whose marriage had been a diplomatic match; she is said to have sobbed at the prospect of a husband with hunched back, large nose and piercing eyes, yet in time the marriage proved to be a happy and loving one.

Now, however, what would become known as the War of the Spanish Succession, colloquially the Marlborough Wars, became inevitable, and across Europe enlistment was in full swing, including in Ireland. William III appointed John Churchill, Earl of Marlborough, as Ambassador-Extraordinary in The Hague and as Captain General of the English forces; his specific task was to negotiate a new

Grand Alliance of England, the Netherlands and the Holy Roman Empire to oppose France and Spain. Shortly after this was achieved the unexpected death of William and the accession of Queen Anne threw this alliance into jeopardy.

★ ★ ★

Each winter when King William returned home from the summer campaigning, he enjoyed hunting at Hampton Court Palace; he had established his court at this country estate on account of his lifelong asthma, which had been exacerbated by the frequent fog when he had been in London. On 21 January 1702, he was riding his horse in the Home Park when it tripped over a molehill, causing the king to fall.

William broke his collarbone, a common though painful riding injury; the king was nearly recovered when complications set in, possibly due to asthma, for in early March he caught a pulmonary fever and died in Kensington Palace. His wife, Mary, had died of smallpox back in 1694 and on his death it was discovered he had kept a lock of her hair and her wedding ring next to his heart. After King William's death, however, the Jacobites thereafter drank a toast to 'the little gentleman in black velvet', referring to the mole over whose hill the king had fallen.

So Anne was now queen and she wanted her husband, Prince George of Denmark, to be the new allied commander-in-chief over Marlborough. Queen Anne had a soft voice that was said to be both clear and pleasant; she loved her husband and bore him seventeen children, not one of whom survived into adulthood, and she herself suffered ill health throughout her life. Although her main pastimes were said to be playing cards, drinking tea and admiring gardens, and she was said to have a dislike of fresh air, nonetheless it was while in her chaise and following the royal buckhounds hunting through Windsor Forest that she earmarked a place called Ascot Heath for a racecourse and paid just over £558 for it; the title of 'Royal Ascot' dates from that year, 1711.

Her husband was unpopular, however. While the Allies would just about accept Marlborough being in nominal overall command at the time of Anne's accession in 1702 — subject to their being consulted every step of the way — they detested the thought of a Danish prince being in that position. Luckily, the Queen, a great personal friend at this time of Marlborough's wife, Sarah, relented, and confirmed the position of the Earl.

★   ★   ★

John Churchill had come far since his impoverished Cavalier father, Winston, had despatched him from Devonshire as a page-boy to the court of the Duke of York (the future James II). It had not been success all the way; he had spent a short spell in the Tower of London, supposedly for supporting the restoration of King James II. The accusation was subsequently proved to be false.

In a true love match, Churchill had married Sarah Jennings in 1677; he always thirsted for power, which through his wife's long friendship with the future queen, Anne, he continued to gain. Through his charm, good looks, intelligence and diplomatic powers of persuasion, he had already risen steadily from being an ensign in the Foot Guards of the King's Own Company, serving in battles at sea and on land.

Like so many Englishmen, Churchill abhorred King James II's Catholicism and, as we have seen, he switched allegiance to William when James was encamped at Salisbury, en route to 'greet' William's landing in Devon in 1688.

Churchill's reward from William in 1689 was to be created Earl of Marlborough and promoted to lieutenant-general. In the autumn of 1690 he was responsible for capturing the

135

southern Irish ports of Cork and Kinsale, thus ensuring that the French would be unable to use them to land reinforcements.

But even then his career was not smooth and it was to be ten years before he took command in the field again. In the aftermath of his wife's falling out with Queen Mary, the Marlboroughs were banished from court and the Earl was stripped of his posts. During this time they also lost their youngest child, Charles, before his second birthday, leaving the couple with five daughters and a son.

London's court circles might laugh at the fidelity between them, but nothing could quench their love. It was many years since Churchill had been renowned as an adventurous rake whose reputation was never higher than when he jumped from the chamber of the king's mistress, Barbara Villiers, as King Charles himself approached. But then he had met Sarah, and he had quite simply never looked at another woman.

And so now in 1702 the Earl of Marlborough, in favour under Queen Anne (for the time being at least), was to embark for Holland, to try and persuade the Dutch that it was time to stop shilly-shallying and force the French to fight. By this time, the pike was nearly obsolete, and was phased out by 1704, after which pikemen were issued with firelocks and ring bayonets. The arrival of Marlborough also saw the start of much better discipline among the English regiments.

★ ★ ★

Not only was Kit back in uniform, but within a year she was attracting notice again, this time in military action. She was in a detachment of Horse and Dragoons under Major General Dompre during the siege of the French-occupied, strongly fortified Kaiserswert (today part of Dusseldorf), in May 1702. Suddenly they came upon the vanguard of the enemy and found themselves in a skirmish against a superior number of French cavalry who were 'very rough' with them. Kit, in the thick of the fighting, had to use all her wits, doubtless striking fearlessly with her sword and holding her horse steady at the same time. She 'had the good fortune, though in the thickest of the engagement, to escape without hurt, and to be taken notice of by the officers'. The French were 'put to the run with considerable loss, and very little on the English'.

There is no reason to suppose that Kit did not join in with her comrades off duty — indeed, we know she did so on occasions such as when she was propositioned by the prostitute — and so we can imagine her unwinding with a mug of beer after the action, and hearing what had gone on in other parts of the field as stories were swapped. Being better educated and probably more interested than most, we can suppose she was told about the goings on at Nijmegen, which had suffered a surprise attack by the French.

'They were trying to draw us away from Kaiserswert,' Lieutenant Keith may have told her.

'What happened?' Kit quaffed her beer, glad of the refreshment, wiping some of the grime off her face with her free hand.

A drummer was practising close by and several men crowded around Lieutenant Keith, trying to listen to the story.

'Wait till you hear. Being a Sunday Nijmegen wasn't expecting 'visitors',' he said, unbuttoning his coat and spreading his legs over a nearby stool. 'It had no cannons on the ramparts; the magazines were locked up and then they couldn't find the keys. The guards were away from their posts, and most of the inhabitants were listening to church sermons — and believe me they would be long and . . . '

'Dull,' Kit finished for him. 'So how did they save themselves?' The sutler poured out more beers for the men, and hovered while waiting to be paid.

'The burghers heard the alarm first and rushed to their arms,' Lieutenant Keith continued. 'Apparently they broke open the magazines, drew out the cannon by themselves, and shot at the French — damned brave of the old boys, don't you think?'

Kit nodded.

'Anyway, Boufflers wasn't expecting that sort of defence; he was forced to retreat.'

'Good for them.' Kit remembered the time she had been grateful to a town burgher. 'Anyway at least we've seen some action, might lift the men's spirits a bit.'

'I wouldn't bank on it,' Lieutenant Keith said. 'Those damned Dutch field deputies are so cautious.' A prostitute wandered by, eyeing them up; Kit turned the other way. When she'd gone by, Keith said, 'You never know who's a spy. But those deputies, I tell you they're just bloody civilians, yet they have full powers over the Dutch part of the army and they keep on vetoing attack.'

'How often?'

'Four times this August alone!' He took another draught of beer. 'No wonder the men are so fed up.'

★　★　★

Kit's intermittent efforts at finding her 'brother' continued in vain and finally she concluded that Richard must be dead. In an effort to forget him she 'took recourse to wine and company, as the melancholy of remembering him did nothing for him and consumed me'. This 'had the desired effect and the season passed pretty cheerfully'. So she again threw herself into the life of a serving soldier. She learnt a lot more about how to take risks in order to make money during her second period in active army life. So often matters came down to money.

She also had her own horse to care for and her natural affinity came to the fore; she may have become a tough, hard soldier but underneath she was still a horse-loving girl; their smell, their power, their selfless loyalty, willingness to please and majestic pace never palled for her.

Sometimes the dragoons were sent out, officially, to forage in the neighbouring countryside. Peasants fearing for their lives fled before them, and in their haste implements were often left behind. One day, Kit's horse trod on an abandoned scythe that was half covered by grass. It sprang up and cut her horse so seriously that Kit despaired of his recovery. Possibly the blade caught an artery in the horse's foreleg. The cut was sharp and deep. Blood spewed, pumping out in a frightening flow, looking all the worse because the horse, like all those in her regiment, was grey. Kit's natural nursing instincts combined with her childhood knowledge of horses would have come to the rescue, and she would have had to stem the flow of blood by tying a tourniquet. For this, she probably tore a strip off her tunic and, with blood flowing profusely, she would have placed a stick in the cloth, placed it above the wound and turned it like a key to wind the cloth ever tighter, until the artery was blocked. A few moments later the horse's knees might have given way as by then no blood was circulating around its body or reaching its brain; immediately, Kit would have released the tourniquet a notch, re-tightened it as blood spurted again, and repeated the process a number of times until finally no more blood escaped through the wound. She records that at length he was again fit for service.

She remembered the date; it was 29 August 1702, and it was during the Siege of Venlo, both town and citadel. The strategically placed town on the River Meuse had once been a Roman settlement; by the ninth century it was known as a trading post, and it was granted city status in 1343. Kit toiled with her comrades in digging the trenches, a task that took six arduous days.

'We assaulted the citadel with success and few of the garrison escaped with life; those that did had not enough rags left for a cut finger.'

Another contemporary soldier, Captain Robert Parker of the Royal Irish Regiment, records the action in far greater detail, explaining that, contrary to normal rules of siege craft, Lord 'Salamander' Cutts pursued the defenders from post to post until his men captured the whole fort. As he put it, 'Thus were the unaccountable orders of Lord Cutts as unaccountably executed, to the great surprise of the whole army and even of ourselves when we came to reflect on what we had done'.

Warfare at this time was carried out according to codes of conduct accepted by both sides, and this sort of slaughter on an already defeated opponent was not part of them.

Captain Parker continued: 'Had not several unforeseen accidents occurred, not a man of us could have escaped. In particular, when we had penetrated as far as the wooden bridge, had the officer drawn the loose plank after him, as he ought, we must all have fallen into the moat which was ten feet deep in water.'

★   ★   ★

After the action the victors took part in the traditional pillaging, looting and raping, Kit amongst them except, of course, in the latter activity. She and her comrades climbed the 600 steps to the citadel, stepping over bodies on the way, only to find the Grenadiers had got there before them and bagged the first choice. Among the items left lying around there were 30 pieces of cannon and 20,000 silver florins. Kit set about grabbing what she could and emerged with a large silver chalice and pieces of plate.

She records that she afterwards sold the booty 'to a Dutch Jew for a third part of their value'. Such merchants typically followed at the rear of the army in those times for just such deals. On her next trip Kit found some good wine, excellent bread and a quantity of meat. With an eye as ever to keeping in with her superiors, she took much of this to some of her officers' tents.

★ ★ ★

Winter quarters were in Venlo for the likes of Kit, billeted on unwilling and sometimes resentful residents and innkeepers. Marlborough, meanwhile, headed for The Hague and home, back to the politics of the day, and Sarah's arms; but he nearly did not make it.

He was being escorted by Venlo's Governor by boat along the Meuse, with a mounted escort accompanying him along the banks, Kit among them.

As they rode in darkness Kit came upon a hog sty containing a sow with five piglets, one of which Kit took herself. She had it for some time when one Corporal Taylor from Brigadier Panton's Regiment tried to take it off her.

Not surprisingly, this caused words between them which developed into a fight. The corporal drew his sword and made a swipe at Kit's head; she fended it off with her hands and the sinew of her little finger was cut in two. She grabbed the butt end of her pistol and struck him between the eyes.

While this was happening much worse was taking place up ahead, for most of Marlborough's escort was lost in the dark and fog and suddenly the Earl and his officers found themselves surrounded by 35 French soldiers, some of them Irish mercenaries.

News of this calamity spread through the entire army and none was more stricken than the Governor of Venlo. Putting himself at the head of the men, he marched straight to Guelders, threatening dire extremities if Marlborough was not delivered up at once. Marlborough was not recognised by his captors and showed a sham pass belonging to his younger brother,

Charles Churchill; but it was out of date and it was only after hours of negotiation in which lesser men, including his chef, were taken prisoner that Marlborough was freed.

Once the Governor of Venlo heard that Marlborough was safe, to his immense relief and that of the men, he marched back again. When Marlborough finally reached The Hague he was given a massive reception, the people there still believing him to be captured. Once home, Queen Anne bestowed on Marlborough the titles Marquis of Blandford and Duke of Marlborough. He was 52 years old; and the most daring action of his career was as yet an embryonic secret plan.

★　★　★

Back in camp bonfires blazed, hogs roasted and the whole camp joined in the celebrations and revelry at the news that their 'Corporal John' — for they thought of him as 'one of us' — had been made a duke. His elevation was to cause some jealousy back in England, but to his troops he was revered.

After her fracas with Corporal Taylor, Kit got her little finger sewn up; the fate of the pig is unrecorded, but the Corporal's eye was struck out and he was paid out by his company. Four years later, at the Siege of

145

Lille, Kit recorded that he lost it all at play and shot himself through the head.

After the celebrations, it was back to gambling, drinking, whoring and playing cards and dice when not on military duty in winter quarters. Drilling continued throughout the winter. A number of officers would be back in England, Scotland and Ireland recruiting new men and as they arrived they had to learn all the rules, and take the extra drilling, just as Kit had done.

Kit thought of Richard once more: 'As we lay quiet all the winter, my husband, whom the hurry of the war had in a manner banished, occurred to my memory, and I made what enquiry I could after him, but in vain; wherefore, I endeavoured, as I concluded him for ever lost, to forget him, as the melancholy the remembrance of him brought upon me, profited him nothing, while it consumed me. To do this, I had recourse to wine and company, which had the effect I wished, and I spent the season pretty cheerfully.'

The following summer, 1703, there were a number of sieges and skirmishes, but the Allies failed in their attempts to bring the enemy to a battle and, in Kit's words, 'did nothing more than observe the enemy' for the rest of the campaign.

* * *

In England the following winter Marlborough was working long into the night by candlelight. The war was unpopular in England, and he felt that he was destined to another season of inactivity unless he could come up with something outstanding.

There was alarm amongst the Allies at the ambitions of the Elector of Bavaria, Maximilian Emanuel; it was known he wanted his dynasty to supplant the Habsburgs as Holy Roman Emperors, and he had the support of the French.

In Marlborough's time the Holy Roman Empire made up the triumvirate of allies, along with the Dutch and British, who fought the French in the War of the Spanish Succession. If Bavaria, backed by France, succeeded in gaining a foothold in the Holy Roman Empire it would leave open the road to Vienna, and if that happened, the Holy Roman Empire would be forced into a separate peace that would weaken the Alliance disastrously. As it was, there were already many in England who denounced the war, claiming France was impregnable.

In the Holy Roman Empire a free imperial city was a city formally ruled by the emperor only, as opposed to the majority of cities in the Empire, which were governed by one of the many princes of the Empire, such as dukes or prince-bishops. One such was Prince Eugene of Savoy; he was President of the Imperial War Council and was to become a personal friend as well as close ally of Marlborough. Prince Eugene and Count Wratsilaw, the imperial ambassador in London, together realised how imperilled Vienna had become, and they laid the initial foundation to Marlborough's plan.

When Queen Anne sent the Duke of Marlborough back to the Low Countries in 1704 it was with the instruction to go to the aid of Austria, if he saw fit. This was exactly the encouragement he needed, and was in time to boost the morale of officers and men alike.

★   ★   ★

Before he travelled, Marlborough sat pondering at the bureau in his Holywell home, near St Alban's; he knew he must come up with a plan that was at once both daring and bold. Surprise was the key, and it was virtually impossible to keep anything a surprise from the enemy when so many Dutch field deputies had to be consulted, and they in turn had to consult each other, and by the time they had decided upon any course

— usually a negative one — the spies had long since got news of it to the French. So Marlborough would consult only a hand-picked few — and even then, he might not tell them the *whole* truth.

He scrutinised a map of Europe, noting yet again the vital river systems and the positions held by the enemy. Something niggled in his brain . . . It was after midnight before Marlborough put away the maps, his furrowed brow giving way to a small smile.

He had the solution to the vexed war question in his head, and he would act upon it with all the expediency he could muster.

12

The Long March

Thump, thump, swish. Thump, thump, swish. Kit strapped her horse rhythmically with long, firm strokes. She stood back and admired the bulging grey muscles, twisted more straw into her hand and continued with the grooming. Nearby, she could hear soldiers whistling as they wielded their axes at the young trees; their sergeant was helping them and sharing their jokes. Throughout the camp, as men went about their duties and chores, there was an air of anticipation; whether collecting water, chopping firewood, cooking in groups around a fire, or even drilling, the men's eyes were brighter: there was to be a goal, something to strive for.

Had they known what Marlborough really had in mind, even they might have jibbed.

★ ★ ★

Marlborough kept his secret well. Not only was it important to keep the enemy guessing and confused, but had he told the whole

Allied army of his unique, 'unthinkable' plan, he might not have carried them with him. Instead, he had merely hinted, in a February visit to The Hague, of a campaign on the Moselle. Master diplomat that Marlborough was, he managed to persuade the reluctant Dutch to leave their troops where they were in southern Germany, and to allow them to join him in his campaign. Crucially, he also received Dutch permission to go on the Moselle campaign himself.

It was not until 29 April 1704 that Marlborough told Sidney Godolphin, Lord Treasurer of England and later Earl of Godolphin in 1706, of his real plans; even his wife Sarah, confidante of the Queen, was kept in the dark. To the troops and friend and foe alike, with the exception of Godolphin, Prince Eugene of Savoy and Count Wratislaw, the Moselle was the destination.

And that would be no mean undertaking in itself.

★   ★   ★

In camp, Kit and Lieutenant Keith struck their tent and packed and loaded their baggage, along with the rest of their comrades. They marched up through Holland, reaching Begburg two weeks later on 12 May, where they joined their Prussian allies, swelling the army to some 21,000 men. Pouring rain made the ground of the vast encampment thick with mud but the men strode through it with a will; they relished the thought of action at last.

First, they were to be inspected by Marlborough himself.

★ ★ ★

Marlborough sat astride his magnificent white horse and surveyed the massed ranks spread out over the plain. It looked like a sparkling sea, with the light glinting on swords and stirrups, bits and buttons. Judging by contemporary illustrations, he would have held his horse lightly in his left hand as he sat erect in the deep leather saddle, doffing his hat with his right as he walked his steed slowly along the lines, stopping for a word here and a pleasantry there, not just with the colonels, but with the men, too, whose eyes shone with pride.

Marlborough was the epitome of a born leader. His dark eyes shone beneath his gold-braided tricorne hat. Some of the long fair curls of his wig fell forward over his shoulders and the rest ran straight down his upright back. His scarlet frock coat was braided in gold along the facings, around the cuffs, over the shoulders and in impressive lines down the back vents, ending with gold trimmings spread out over his horse's hindquarters. Peeping from beneath the coat skirt was his gold-hilted sword, while strapped to the horse's shoulder was the gold-and-crimson-embroidered horse housing containing his silver-mounted flintlock pistols in their holster caps. The splatter-dashes, a recent innovation that kept the mud off his shoes and lower legs, were fastened with gold buttons the whole way down, and his rowelled spurs and stirrup irons were of gold, too. For someone who would soon be 54, he looked remarkably young, with a fair complexion almost devoid of wrinkles. Today he felt young, too, as he processed slowly from regiment to regiment, inspecting and encouraging the men.

The inspection lasted most of the morning and, as Marlborough rode back to his waiting coach, there was not a man on that broad plain who did not swear by him.

★   ★   ★

The rest of the day was spent in packing and loading. The camp resembled a huge ants' nest with figures scurrying in every direction;

like ants, there was nothing random in their movements and strict discipline was maintained throughout. The officers labelled and weighed their own baggage, overseen by one of the non-commissioned officers, who charged them for any bags that were overweight, before placing them on the waiting transport. The supplies for each regiment were also placed on carts, along with the arms and store chests and officers' personal baggage; small boxes were allowed for the non-commissioned officers, but no private boxes or packages were permitted — any found that had been secreted onto the wagons were destroyed.

It was different for Marlborough: his personal allowance was 27 wagons, 3 carts and 20 baggage horses.

★   ★   ★

It was dawn. No reveille was called; instead, the assembly drum beat, indicating the march was shortly to begin. Soon Kit, like the rest of her comrades, was dressed and ready in her uniform, her horse held lightly in her hand and her back erect, awaiting the signal to march.

Her horse wore an embroidered cloth under the saddle; also strapped to her were a bucket, forage bags, ropes and pegs, plus camp equipment that was shared out between the men. Kit slung a leather bucket for her musket over her shoulder, and strapped a saddle-bag containing her personal items to her back. As usual, her sword hung by her side.

★   ★   ★

Richard, like his fellow infantrymen, would have slung his own belongings and his share of camp equipment — kettle, pick-axe, shovel, tent-poles and the like — in the bag over his shoulder along with his musket and water container; and his sword hung from the sword belt at his waist. He probably grimaced, unable to share in the air of anticipation around him. How often did he still think of Kit? Did he still yearn for her?

★   ★   ★

Now, at the appointed hour, the drummers beat a march at the head of the line.

Ninety squadrons of horse wheeled in impressively behind them, manes and tails flowing, bridles clinking, soldiers' gold-laced red coats blazing, plumes from tricorne hats flying. They were followed by 51 battalions of infantry, firelocks shouldered, buttons shining, leather shoes polished. This mass of humanity wheeled into place in an orderly, disciplined fashion, with little noise beyond the beating of the drums, the clinking of the arms and the footsteps on the earth. The long march, as it became known, had begun.

★   ★   ★

They marched in silence, and large gaps between the divisions were not allowed. Officers were required to march in their posts and all sergeants and soldiers had to remain in rank and file, mass discipline that helped maintain good order.

To finance the march, Godolphin furnished Marlborough with enough gold, which was conveyed in heavily guarded coffers, known collectively as the Military Chest. At this stage there were about 2,000 cavalry horses (more would join them along the route), plus some 5,000 wagon horses to pull 1,700 supply carts, and the same number again pulling the artillery train (even so, the heavy cannon were left behind); so feed had to be provided for 12,000 horses on the march as well as for the men. Thanks to Marlborough's meticulous planning and network of contacts, along with hard cash as opposed to promises, they were well supplied.

The wagons, known as Marlbrouks, were

specially designed to cope with the rough terrain, and carried a range of munitions and supplies for both men and horses. Lesser criminals were handcuffed in the middle of the provost's guard, and secured in the strongest house available at night, as were the serious offenders who were chained hand and foot and conveyed in the bread wagons.

These travelled at the rear of the army along with the sutlers' carts, and the wagons for guns and powder, along with any camp followers, such as soldiers' wives, mistresses *et al*. Baggage wagons moved off every two hours, and carried those who were too ill to march. The heavy goods were transported by waterways, first along the River Meuse, and then the Rhine, enabling fair speed to be made.

And speed was of the essence. The enemy must be kept wrong-footed for as long as possible.

The first day over, the men pitched their tents once more. Kit noticed that Lord Hay and newly promoted Lieutenant Colonel George Preston ensured their regiment was safely encamped before leaving for more salubrious lodgings, in nearby houses. Captain Thomas Young and his subalterns ensured all the men's tents were up before pitching their own.

★ ★ ★

Richard would have found this part of the march easy; the terrain was similar to that of the previous war and was easy to negotiate, mostly on flat causeways flanked by growing corn or grazing cattle; it was criss-crossed by poplar-lined dykes and occasional rivers, outlying farmsteads and villages.

Each morning camp was struck before dawn and at first light they began marching in three columns, covering 12 to 15 miles until about 9 a.m., when they arrived at their next night's stop. There, he and his mates invariably found provisions already laid on for them, leaving them at leisure for the rest of the day.

Initial heavy rain gave way to sun and drought as they travelled west, parallel with the Rhine as far as the spa town of Sinzig; from there they remained close beside the Rhine, marching south towards Coblenz. Picturesque villages and apple orchards lined the riverbanks, and above, on the steep-sided hills, the Rhine was guarded by fairytale-like castles. More pretty German girls turned out to cheer them along the tracks that passed for roads. Spirits and morale were high so that the soldiers swung along good-temperedly, and when camped for the remains of the day

Richard probably joined in with the others. They laughed, swore, drank and joked, enjoying light-hearted banter and the latest rumour-mongering.

Kit enjoyed the stops where various German principalities plied the soldiers with food and beer or wine, as well as fodder for the horses. And they supplied their own troops along the way, too, swelling Marlborough's army with more German, Danish and Prussian men.

At each of these stops, Marlborough let the particular prince into the secret of where he was really heading. By the end of May, most of them knew the truth, including the King of Prussia — previously the Elector Frederick William II, he was allowed by Vienna to take the title of king in return for his support of the Allies — but it was not until the first week of June that the Dutch States General were finally informed.

As far as the troops were concerned, and even the officers, they still believed their destination to be the Moselle.

On 25 May they reached Coblenz. As she rode towards the city on her grey horse Kit looked in wonder at the two mighty rivers, the Moselle and the Rhine; they dwarfed Dublin's River Liffey as they embraced this ancient city. She discovered it had once been a Roman settlement, established between 10 and 8 BC. Both rivers had castles towering over them from high up on steep, densely wooded sides. On the far side the hill below the fortress Ehrenbreitstein resembled a cliff.

Kit could see river transport so that meant the rivers were navigable, and she admired a medieval stone bridge that crossed the Moselle; these features would be important if the city was to be the campaign's chief supply source.

But to the men's surprise, they spent only two days in Coblenz, just enough time for their numbers to be swelled by more Prussian and Hanoverian troops, and they were then ordered to cross the rivers.

Kit must have looked in horror below her. The old bridge across the Moselle was all right. But before it, the engineers had laid pontoons end to end across the Rhine, and they were bobbing up and down. It would be a precarious crossing for both men and horses. Did she remember her youthful rides, smoothly jumping the fences across the Leixlip farm? The pontoons, by contrast, were wobbly and unstable.

★　★　★

From that moment everything changed. There had to be something momentous ahead and rumours were rife among men and officers alike. Were they heading for Alsace?

The French had re-routed from the Moselle Valley to Alsace, so they evidently thought so. Word also had it that two of the French commanders, Marshal Villeroy and Count Tallard, had linked up, complete with a fresh supply of recruits. Maybe Bavaria was the destination. Or was Marlborough simply playing with them?

★ ★ ★

After Coblenz there was no longer a riverside path. The troops had to turn into the sharp inclines of the wooded hillsides a few miles south of the city at Braubach where the steep land around was terraced in the local yellow-grey stone supporting tiny vineyards. It was here that Marlborough went on ahead with the Horse, sending messages back at intervals advising the Foot of the best route to take and those to avoid.

Richard must have looked in horror at the steepness of the hill above Braubach. The columns of men already climbing resembled a swarm of ladybirds with their red coats and packs across their backs. It would soon be his turn to scale it.

The weather turned to continuous rain.

Once it started it did not stop and a soldier, Private John Marshall Deane, wrote, 'It hath rained 32 days together more or less, and miserable marches we have had for deep and dirty roads, and through tedious woods and wildernesses, and over vast high rocks and mountains, that it may be easily judged what our little army endured, and what unusual hardship they went through'.

Their every need was attended to, including, famously, the provision of new shoes for the infantry when needed. And Marlborough more than once gave a lift in his coach to struggling or hobbling soldiers who had fallen by the wayside.

★   ★   ★

The pine needles formed a thick, soft carpet underfoot and they muffled the sound of the horses' footsteps. The forest was so dense that it was as dark as night and the men's chatter and profanities (which they uttered as they rode along when not being watched over) dwindled and then ceased. The eerie silence must have struck Kit as strange, and then she realised what it was: never before had she been in a wood so bereft of life; there was nothing, no birdsong — no birds as far as she could see — not even any sign of deer; there would not be enough for them to eat, just miles and miles of tall pines and the tracks made between them by the advancing army.

Occasionally there was a shaft of light made by a fallen conifer, and only then a few brave flowers peeked out. They came across a stream burbling its way down the mountain that Kit's troop was riding up. She longed to get off, and cup her hands to drink and splash her face, and to let her horse nibble at the patch of grass. Somehow the rain managed to make its way through the mass of trees; Kit breathed in the pungent smell of pine heightened by the wet, and cursed the large raindrops that found a gap at the back of her neck.

*   *   *

During this period of rain the swelling army marched roughly along the Rhine, past one tributary, the River Main at Mainz, and on towards another, the Neckar. Here, in the Alsace region of the southern Rhine near Heidelberg Marlborough ordered a bridge of boats to be built across the mighty river at Philippsburg. It was a feint, designed to draw the enemy that way, for, ignoring his bridge, Marlborough instead made yet another unexpected move; he wheeled his army left, heading east. So that was it! The news spread through the camp like a Chinese whisper: Marlborough was bringing his men all the way to the Danube. Would — could — his unprecedented ploy pay off?

★   ★   ★

The French generals Villeroy and Tallard watched the manoeuvre. François de Neufville, Duc de Villeroy, was a member of Louis XIV's inner circle and was appointed Marshal of France by him in 1693. A polished courtier and leader of society, he was also known as a man of great personal gallantry. Camille d'Hostun de la Baume, Due de Tallard was a French noble, diplomat and military commander, who also became Marshal of France, in 1703. After the Nine Years' War (in which Kit first served) he was Ambassador at St James's Palace; when Louis XIV recognised James, the Old Pretender, as rightful monarch of what had been the Stuart kingdoms, William III expelled him from London, shortly before the start of the War of the Spanish Succession.

Now the truth of Marlborough's destination finally became clear to these two French leaders. Marlborough was going to try and prevent the Elector of Bavaria from taking

Vienna and placing himself on the Imperial throne. The French chiefs scurried to send messages back to their king at Versailles.

* * *

Marlborough rode on, proud of the men he was leading, and arranged a rendezvous to discuss plans with Prince Eugene at the village of Mundelsheim on the edge of the Black Forest. The Prince had already arrived with his army of 28,000 men.

Prince Eugene of Savoy had one purpose in life: to defeat the French. His Italian mother was raised in France and probably had designs on marrying Louis XIV, before finally marrying Eugene's father, Eugene, Prince of Savoy; the couple had eight children and Eugene, born in Paris, was the fifth son and was brought up in the French court at Versailles. His father was mostly away campaigning in the French army and died in 1673 when Eugene was ten, and his mother, Olympia, who had a reputation for impropriety, left the country under a cloud, leaving Eugene and his younger sisters to be brought up by their paternal grandmother and aunt.

Louis XIV had Eugene earmarked to be a priest. Eugene wanted to be a soldier but his protests fell on deaf ears so, determined and independent of character, he escaped Versailles and travelled to Vienna; an older brother had been killed in the service of Austria, and Prince Louis of Baden, a first cousin, was a general in the Imperial army.

As G. M. Trevelyan observed, 'Louis never did a worse day's work for the French army.' Eugene was unmarried and channelled all his energy to his given cause. His military career was to span 50 years, and before this first meeting with Marlborough he had already conquered the Turks; successfully taken an army across the Alps; and generally combined zeal with intelligence.

★ ★ ★

The 40-year-old Prince Eugene, accompanied by Prince Wratislaw, rode towards the Duke of Marlborough at the head of the huge camp in Mundelsheim, a village lying in the upper reaches of the Neckar midway between the Rhine and the Danube. It was 5 p.m. on 10 June 1704, and, remarkably, it was the first time Eugene and Marlborough had ever met. Their liking towards each other was instant; they 'clicked'. According to the memoirs of Captain Robert Parker, the two men 'contracted an extraordinary friendship for each other; and it held to the last'. This boded well for the task that lay ahead.

The best silver plate was set for a lavish dinner for the two men; two days later they moved on to Grossheppach where, keen to show off his forces to his new best friend, Marlborough paraded all 19 squadrons of the English cavalry for Prince Eugene to review. One can imagine Marlborough's chest swelling with near father-like pride as the meadows between the Neckar and Mundelsheim village glowed scarlet with more than 2,000 horsemen lined up in front of the younger man, Kit among them; she and her comrades probably considered themselves best of them all, mounted as they were on their grey horses. After all the wet weather, there was now a spell of glorious summer, and the cavalry shimmered in the sunshine. As Prince Eugene noted, 'While English money could purchase the finest horses and smartest uniforms, the evident bon viveur and smiles on the men's faces could not be bought'.

Two days after this impressive review, on 14 June, the two men met Eugene's cousin, Prince Louis, Margrave of Baden, under a tree outside the Lamb Inn in Grossheppach; a bronze memorial commemorates the meeting.

Here, these three most important men of the Allied campaign could not be overheard. It was imperative for them to see eye to eye.

This was the meeting at which they decided who should be in charge of what, leading up to and during the pending conflict. There was never going to be any dispute or competition between Eugene and Marlborough, and Eugene readily agreed to go to the Rhine with his force of nearly 30,000 men, there to keep the larger forces of Tallard and Villeroy 'amused' for as long as it took Marlborough to steal yet another march on them on his way to the Danube.

It was agreed that Prince Louis would hold back the Bavarians near Ulm, and that Marlborough would march to him, to join their two armies; it was further agreed that he and Marlborough would lead this huge joint army on alternate days. But in practice, Marlborough would prove to be the real commander.

13

Injured in Action

The storm struck the day Richard and his comrades headed for the two-mile-long Geislingen Pass, one of several that had been old Roman trading routes through the Jura Mountains. The steep incline would not usually have posed a problem to a marching army, but what happened was hardly normal. It took two days for the infantry to cross; one hill took up a whole day.

At first, there was more heavy rain, drenching the men within moments, and then the hail began. The chatter between men was at first in wonderment at the size of the hailstones but as the storm progressed, with flashes of lightning and wind howling so fiercely that trees bent double, and the hailstones the size of large coins or small pebbles smashed into their faces, they became silent, unable to speak. Within half an hour of the storm beginning the mud was over their ankles, and new rivulets sent torrents of water down their paths. Shoes were lost. Straining horses floundered, traces snapped. Wagons got stuck, or overturned in the morass.

Richard might have been among those ordered to help move a wagon, one of several that was stuck fast. The lead horse was down on its knees. They were told to 'put your shoulders to the wheel'.

One man would have taken hold of the lead horse's bridle and pulled at the stricken creature's head, while his comrades tried bodily to lift the wheels out of ruts that were two feet deep. Richard would have cursed the 50 lb weight of his pack upon his back.

The men cursed more as they slipped and slid through the deep mud, pushing and pulling their equipment through the quagmire. The hail stung their faces; they grabbed at their tricornes as the wind nearly swept them off their heads. Just at that moment the horse lurched forward, lost his legs again, and fell in a heap against Richard, knocking him into the soft ground. Richard curled himself into a ball and rolled away from the thrashing legs; he felt one kick to his back but it was protected by the heavy pack which he had been cursing only moments earlier. Already soaked to the skin, he was now caked in mud, too. It was going to be some time before he could reach the warmth of the campfire and a chance to dry out his uniform and warm his weary body.

At last the storm abated, but the rain continued and the temperature dropped. Marlborough was aware of the plight of his men in these conditions. The rain brought with it cold so severe that he had a stove lit in his chamber. Writing to Sarah, and telling her of the fire, he noted 'but the poor men that have not such convenience, I am afraid will suffer from the continual rain'. He added that although 'the rains do us hurt here, they do good to Prince Eugene on the Rhine [by immobilising the French] so that we must take the bad with the good'.

Private John Marshal Deane wrote in his journal of 'a most horrible storm of thunder and lightning and hail and rain. The hail was of such biggness that the whole army was amazed at it. The worst day's march that ever the oldest soldier alive ever marched, for there was a steep, rocky mountain about half a league high, and after; a deep clay rode and occasioned by the stormy weather that we could hardly get our legs out of the earth.'

But another soldier, Donald McBane, a 'rascally' grenadier and noted swordsman, described the march in more positive terms. 'We set out for Germany and had seven weeks' march, but had plenty of good bread and wine, and the people were very kind to us along the Rhine.'

★   ★   ★

On 22 June the Allies reached the plateau above Ulm. Kit caught her breath; below them, in the distance, she could see the majestic Danube flowing between flat meadows. The men made a comparatively easy descent and five days later they reached the banks of the Danube at the outskirts of Donauworth: the end of their epic long march.

It had taken six weeks and they had covered some 250 miles since they started from Begburg. But in spite of some gruelling phases, the men were fit, well and in good humour. They needed to be, for that very evening they were in action, storming the Schellenberg Heights.

★   ★   ★

'No, Sir, don't make me leave.' Musket shots were raining down. Kit straightened herself in an effort to hide the injury. Her blood was up in the thick of the battle for the Schellenberg Heights. More musket balls flew through the air. Leaves fell prematurely to the ground and

172

the clash of steel on steel made it hard to hear orders.

The battle was necessary to force a passage over the Danube to establish a secure forward base, placing the Allies between the French army and Vienna, and to secure a safe supply route from the friendly German states. The enemy was still in the process of fortifying the Schellenberg Heights, and it was imperative for Marlborough to take it before they had completed those fortifications, no matter that it was straight after the arduous march; he had complete faith in them.

★   ★   ★

As dragoons, Kit and her comrades had cut and bundled quantities of sticks, 'fascines', which were given to the advance infantry to lay down on wet or muddy ground and to fill in ditches to ease the way for the rest of the army. Kit and her fellows were ordered to dismount and fight on foot for the second assault, remounting later in the day for the third and final assault — but by then without Kit.

It was no easy victory. Twice the Allies advanced and twice they were beaten back. Robert Parker recorded that 'the hill was in itself steep and very rough, and difficult to ascend, beside which they had thrown up an entrenchment on the summit of it'. It was only at length that the enemy gave way, 'and a terrible slaughter ensued, no quarter being given for a long time'.

A musket ball caught General Goor between his eyes; Monsieur Mortaigne ran to assist, but the General died instantly in his arms. The Duke of Lunebourg Bevern was killed. General William Cadogan had his horse killed under him. The bloody battle continued to rage as Captain Young repeated his order to Kit: 'You must leave the field.'

'No, Sir, please,' Kit implored. 'They need me.' Kit had been hit in the thigh by a musket ball during the second attack, when they were on foot.

Reluctantly, the young captain seconded two soldiers to lift Kit and place her under a tree. It was the last time she saw him. But for now, with her back propped against a tree and her tunic wound around her hip, blood seeping through the hole made in the top of her breeches by the musket shot, she cheered on her comrades animatedly.

'Kill them! Kill, kill, kill the bastards!' she roared. Others cried, 'God Save the Queen.' All around her was noise as her colleagues advanced swiftly on foot and shouting at the top of their voices so loudly that a French officer, Colonel de la Colonie, later recorded that 'the rapidity of the movements together with their loud yells, were truly alarming'. He tried to counter this by ordering the French drums to beat to drown their noise. 'Rage, fury and desperation were manifested by both sides.' The hand-to-hand fighting was fierce, the French hurling back the Allies as they clutched at the parapet. According to Colonel de la Colonie, a French officer, 'men were slaying or tearing at the muzzles of guns and at the bayonets which pierced their entrails'.

The Allies attacked for a third time, while Kit remained under the tree, and at last she saw them get into the trenches and beat down the foe — but, she wrote, 'It was a dear bought victory as they had to dispute every inch of ground and the men showed uncommon bravery.'

Lying strewn around her, dead, were many of the men she had been sharing her life with in camp and on the march and some had become good friends, some of her officers, too. Now, as she was placed on a stretcher, she heard that Captain Young, Captain Douglass and Lieutenant Maltary were among those killed.

Captain John Blackader of the Cameronian Regiment later recorded that 'the carcasses were very thick strewed upon the ground, naked and corrupting . . . seeing the bodies of our comrades and friends lying as dung upon the face of the earth.'

Also on the casualty list was Prince Lewis, the Margrave of Baden, who had been injured in the foot; he died nearly three years later from the wound, in January 1707.

This one battle saw the greatest loss of Allied officers throughout the long War of the Spanish Succession. In all, six lieutenant-generals, four major generals and twenty-eight brigadiers and colonels perished on the Schellenberg Heights.

In all, the Allies had lost 3,000 killed and wounded. From the Greys seven troopers were killed and 17 wounded, including Kit.

And so Dragoon 'Christopher' Welsh, who had been in the thick of battle, was now being carried to hospital in Nordlingen. There she was placed under three surgeons, Messrs Wilson, Laurence and Sea. Did she bite her tongue to fight back a need to scream as the surgeons probed the open wound, or was she more concerned that her sex would be discovered? Did having gone through the pain of childbirth three times help her bear the agony now? Perhaps she instinctively found herself breathing rapidly, clutching at the sheets, groaning deeply. Just as she thought she could bear no more of the pain and the probing, and the scraping of flayed flesh, one of the surgeons stood back, and gave his opinion to his colleagues.

'There's nothing more to be done; it's gone too deep and is lodged between two bones. The ball will have to stay there. It may in due course work its way to the surface.'

He turned on his heel, the others following, leaving an orderly to apply a mixture of spirit of nitre and mercury, with the aim of preventing gangrene, and dressed the wound as best he could.

Kit recorded that 'it remained an open wound for the rest of my life. It almost deprived me of the use of my leg . . . and my sex only narrowly escaped discovery'.

At least she didn't suffer the fate of some of those around her who lost limbs. Maybe next to her was a comrade who was not so lucky, his lower leg sticking out at right angles from the rest of his body; it was not a clean break for the limb had been mashed just below the knee. Not only that, but it was swollen and in colour it was a mix of purple and black. The wound stank.

The surgeon approached him with a rudimentary operating palette, including a razor blade, assorted knifes and a saw. The surgeon's mate drew back the bloodied dressing.

The surgeon took one look and said, 'This

isn't a new wound. How long have you had this?' He wound his cravat around his mouth as he spoke, and leant over with his razor, its blade shining in the otherwise dull light. He dug around cursorily and a jet of green-black slime flowed from the wound; he said nothing but his eyes told the patient everything.

Amputation was the only option.

More orderlies would have come in, one wheeling a bin, another holding the patient's arms above his head with one hand and lifting a shot of brandy to the soldier's lips; it would be all the anaesthetic he would get. The surgeon's assistant bound the leg tightly in a bulge two inches above the wound.

The surgeon took his knife and as he cut into the flesh down to the bone both the orderlies held the man down; the surgeon removed the membrane so that there was absolutely nothing but bone beneath his saw, and set to work.

★   ★   ★

In just a few weeks, with the secret of her sex undiscovered and her leg sufficiently recovered, Kit was able to continue with normal military duties. For now, though, there was the usual matter of booty, and she noted that Marlborough yet again showed his sense of fair play and loyalty to all his men: he decreed that plunder should be 'shared impartially among his brave fellow soldiers', which meant that soldiers like Kit 'under cure' in hospital did not lose out.

The plunder in this instance included arms thrown away by the enemy, plus 13 standards and colours, tents, plate, cannon, copper pontoons, munitions and supplies. And once again, Kit sold on her share.

★   ★   ★

Over a month had passed since the battle of the Schellenberg Heights. Marlborough began again to feel those frustrations of delaying tactics that had so dogged him in the Netherlands. This time it was for want of the arrival of Prince Lewis' promised siege train, without which he could not proceed and finish the job he had started on the Heights. He was a long way from home should things go wrong. And with every day's delay, more and more French troops marched ever closer, swelling the ranks of the enemy army further.

For the men, that month of July was spent razing most of the local villages and small towns to the ground. According to Robert Parker, some 372 towns, villages and farmhouses were burnt to cinders.

It was a practice that Marlborough personally disapproved of because of the devastation it caused to the innocent local populace, leaving most of them ruined and causing the majority to flee to the cities. But it ensured there were little or no growing provisions or stored goods for the enemy to get hold of. It was also retaliation for the Elector of Bavaria's decision to side with the French — it was his land that was being razed. Nevertheless the stress of overseeing this, along with the high losses at Schellenberg, caused Marlborough to suffer headaches bordering on migraine.

Kit probably heard about it in her hospital bed. Maybe she even smelt burning in the air, and while she was also keen to obtain, and sell, booty, it is doubtful that she would have cared for the wholesale laying to waste of good land, practical farmer that she had once been.

★   ★   ★

At last, the prospect of a decisive battle was increasing. Kit was back in her regiment and able to ride. On 5 August, Tallard's forces finally reached those of Marsin and the Elector of Bavaria at Biberach, south of Ulm.

Seeing this, Prince Eugene left part of his army behind on the Rhine, to bluff Villeroy, successfully, into remaining in place.

The next day, Eugene rode over to Marlborough's camp to reconnoitre the surrounding country, for now the opposing armies were only 20 miles apart; nevertheless Marlborough and Eugene sent Prince Lewis off with 20,000 men to besiege Ingolstadt. Either they had great confidence in themselves or little in Lewis — probably the latter.

Eugene's own army, however, was heavily outnumbered, and the French leaders, not realising how closely Eugene and Marlborough kept in touch, thought they could advance upon, and dispose of, Eugene before going on to threaten the main army of Marlborough.

Eugene sensed the danger. Late on the evening of 10 August he sent Marlborough a message that the enemy had marched and had crossed the Danube at Lauingen and that the plain of Dillingen was full of them.

He ended his message with, 'Everything, milord, depends on haste and you get moving straight away in order to join me tomorrow, otherwise I fear it will be too late . . . there is not a moment to lose.'

On receiving this, Marlborough ordered his brother and his troops to go to Eugene's assistance immediately, and for the rest of his army to make ready. With excellent communications between all the commanders, camp was struck and troops assembled in their columns. Within three hours, the main body of the army was on the march, and by late that night, the last of the long columns had crossed to the north bank of the Danube and made camp alongside Eugene at the Schellenberg Heights and along the River Kessel, only three miles from the enemy.

In spite of her wound, Kit was passed fit for active service in what was to prove one of the most famous battles in history.

14

The Big One Looms

John 'Jack' Churchill, Duke of Marlborough, Marquis of Blandford, 'Corporal John' to his men, drew rein on his magnificent white horse.

He and Prince Eugene had ridden out from camp together with an escort to reconnoitre the ground between them and the enemy. They walked and trotted along the little winding roads that crossed the valley meadows around the Danube, and stopped in front of the small white church of Tapfheim. Here, away from prying eyes or listening ears, the two men climbed the steps at the back of the church, paused at the wooden gallery overlooking the nave and chancel, and then climbed the spiral steps until they reached the tiny eyrie at the top. Squashed together, spyglasses in hands, they viewed the surrounding countryside to ascertain the exact whereabouts of the French and to take note of the terrain. What they saw sent pangs quivering through them: a mix of excitement and fear. For there, stretched out on the stubble for four miles in front of them, was the French army going about its business, setting up camp between a little village called Blindheim near the Danube, all the way to the dense pine-clad hills by the village of Lutzingen four miles east. The camp was still being marked out, the white-coated French infantry unhurriedly taking up their appointed stations; foragers were out collecting whatever provisions, fodder and firewood that they could. The rest of the French army could be seen marching to join them; but they were certainly not assembled for battle.

Blindheim, or Blenheim, was a small farming village that had become a fortified stronghold, and was seething with French soldiers. Somehow, Marlborough and Eugene would have to capture it. But the Nebel brook, running alongside the village, appeared to pose an insurmountable obstacle.

Today, the Nebel is little more than a water-filled ditch; in 1704 it was, even undammed, 12 feet wide and surrounded by marsh and reeds (although drier than usual in the hot summer). The French had blocked the two crossings over it, apparently preventing any full frontal attack. Between this and the surrounding terrain, the French seemed to be in a dominant position, and did not believe the Allies would dare to attack.

We can imagine the conversation between the two Allied commanders as they took in the scene from their vantage point in the spire of Tapfheim church.

'If we can cross anywhere then that's where it will have to be.' Marlborough pointed dead ahead to the brook. 'Their wings are too well defended to try any other way. The engineers will have to bridge it with pontoons, and the dragoons with fascines. You, Eugene, will have to take on the French at Lutzingen. The sooner we can engage the enemy while they're still unready, the better.' Marlborough snapped his spyglass shut and spun on his heel. 'Our men can cross that brook!' he declared.

'And I have to deploy my men,' Eugene said. 'There is much work to do.'

'Damn it, that will take time; it's too late to attack today. Pity. But first thing tomorrow, as soon as you have your men there.'

'We'll still surprise them, especially as a reliable source tells me they think we're amassing ready to retreat behind the Danube.'

'The source is sound?'

'Impeccably.'

'That's excellent. For I am told the same.' Marlborough looked Eugene straight in the eye. 'We can cross that brook. We *will* cross it!

'If we can catch them out at first light we

have every chance of beating them — for all that our friend Lewis has gone off looking for glory at Ingoldstadt.'

The two men spoke in unison. 'Thank God!' They had reached the nave of the church they were in; they grinned at each other and embraced. Immediately they were serious again.

Marlborough said, 'God be with you, friend.'

Eugene bowed and said, 'God speed.'

They clasped each other's hands.

★ ★ ★

Marlborough returned to camp and summoned his generals to brief them on the imminent encounter, in particular the plan for crossing the brook and capturing Blenheim. A number of officers voiced their concerns at the wisdom of engaging the enemy in battle because they held the stronger hand. Orkney held his counsel to himself, but had grave misgivings privately; nevertheless, like the other commanders, he would make ready his men. Marlborough and some of the officers sat down to dinner. But he did not feel like eating. Just then, a messenger rushed in, barely knocking, and informed him that his workmen levelling a hollow had been attacked by the enemy.

Already tense, Marlborough stood up and

looked straight at his generals. 'Gentlemen, to your regiments!'

★ ★ ★

1 a.m. Wednesday, 13 August 1704.
The drum beat. It sounded again, a muffled roll; the men must make ready for battle. Did Kit remember that day when she was harvesting the wheat in Leixlip, and the posse came by, kettledrum pounding? And how she used to pretend to be a soldier, snapping imaginary pistols while riding her horse? There was an almost tangible sense of anticipation in camp for the action they all sensed to be imminent.

★ ★ ★

In Blenheim village the previous evening Eugene Jean Philippe, Comte de Mérode-Westerloo, had sat down with fellow officers to a relaxed refreshment of hot soup before retiring to his campaign bed, which had been set up for him in a nearby barn. Tallard was ensconced in the grandest house in the village, while Marsin in Oberglau and the Elector in Lutzingen likewise settled down for a good night's sleep, unconcerned, convinced the Allies were on the point of retreating.

Not one of their spies told them that the Allied officers and men were working like bats in the dark. By 2 a.m. 400 Allied men had been despatched to improve the roads, and 40 squadrons had been sent forward.

Marlborough worked through most of the night. At length, he called Archdeacon Francis Hare, his personal chaplain (and the tutor of his late son), to request the sacraments. The *raison d'être* of his long march had come. Would the gamble pay off? The burden of responsibility weighed heavily on his shoulders at that moment. He lay down for less than two hours.

2 a.m.
George Douglas-Hamilton, Earl of Orkney, ordered his men to clean their arms; it would give them something to do, rather than dwell on the task ahead. Was there something in his demeanour that indicated to his men, Richard among them, that he was not in favour of the imminent conflict? Even men like Richard could see that the French held a superior position.

He and his comrades gathered round for words of comfort, inspiration and God's blessing from one of their regimental chaplains, Jos Loveday. Kit was doubtless fortified in spirit by their chaplain of the Greys, Samuel Noyes, who imparted rousing words of fighting for their queen and country; he was a more reliable chaplain than many, for a high number were often absent without leave.

The blessing enabled Captain Blackader, when marching towards the enemy, to 'exercise a lively faith, relying and encouraging myself in God, whereupon I was easy, sedate, and cheerful'. He firmly believed that his 'angels had me in their charge, and that not a bone should be broken'.

★   ★   ★

3 a.m.

The main Allied force began moving forward in the wake of the 40 squadrons already departed; Marlborough followed behind in his campaign coach. Mist swirled around the men, giving a chill to the August night air.

Just before dawn the Allied army reached Schweningen, two miles from Blenheim. Here, Marlborough and Eugene had one final parley: Marlborough agreed not to attack until he had heard Eugene was safely in place.

And so the force was divided in two. The bulk of Marlborough's men had wound their way in columns to the banks of the Nebel; the mist that surrounded them gave them cover in the first light. They found a goatherd's track through the reeds which made their task a little easier; as a dragoon, Kit was possibly in this advance party, laying fascines to strengthen the footholds in the marsh. Eugene's men marched on. The battle could not begin until he and his men were in place. Everything else was ready: fully dressed and armed men waiting in their regimental companies, the field hospitals, the huge stocks of bread and fodder, and the piles of ammunition. But for Eugene, obstacle after obstacle appeared in his men's path: rougher ground than they had expected, thorn bushes, ditches, streams, boulders — and sporadic enemy fire which, with the Allied cannons being hauled cumbersomely across country, they were not able to return.

7 a.m.
Across the brook all the temporary inhabitants of Blenheim slept soundly in their requisitioned beds, none more so than the French commander, Lieutenant-General the Marquis de Clerambault, who had 16 battalions, including the cream of the French infantry, and 12 squadrons of dragoons within the village, and a further 11 battalions in reserve a few hundred yards away.

Marshal Tallard, officer in command of

Blenheim, also slept deeply. It was doubtless the same in Lutzingen, where the Elector of Bavaria was quartered. In between them, within a musket shot of the Nebel, Marshal Marsin slept in Oberglau, the village right in the centre of the emerging stage for battle.

The story goes that Count Mérode-Westerloo's groom, one Lefranc, rushed to his master, banging on the barn door in Blenheim.

'Sire, the enemy are here!'

Rubbing sleep from his eyes, the Count asked sarcastically, 'Where? Under the bed?'

Lefranc pulled back the curtains around the comfortable camp bed and showed him the sight through the open door. Pulling on his uniform and downing a mug of cocoa, the Count dashed out to his horse and galloped to where Tallard, like the rest of the village and the tented French camp beyond, were still sleeping.

'There was not a single soul stirring as I clattered out of the village.' It was the same when he reached the camp; 'everyone still snug in their tents.'

Tallard peered across the plain; he remained convinced the evident Allied activity was merely preparation for retreat, that they were putting up a smokescreen behind which the main army could disappear with their metaphorical tails between their legs. His aides attempted to inform him to the contrary, and so he summoned Marsin and the Elector.

8–9 a.m.

Now it was the French commanders' turn to climb a church steeple, this time at Blenheim, to view the enemy situation. Tallard, the insignia of the golden fleece around his neck, peered short-sightedly; the Elector and Marsin told him the Allies were preparing for battle. However, they wrongly believed that Baden was on his way to join Marlborough and Eugene which would give the Allies the bigger force; for this reason Tallard suggested that they should defend, rather than attack: to let the Allies come to them. He said that the more of them they let come over the morass, then the more they would be able to kill.

Back in Blenheim, Clerambault was ordered, above all else, to hold the crucial village. The cannon was also fired, ordering the recall of all outposts and foragers, and the villages of Berghausen, Weilheim, and Unterglau were set alight and some other houses near the Nebel, in order to prevent or impede the Allied advance. Marlborough ordered that gun batteries be located upon the most advantageous parts of the ground; he then visited each battery, and stood by to observe the range of the guns and the effect of their fire.

Noon

Had Marlborough not had to wait for Eugene to reach Lutzingen, he could have started battle at first light, with the French not yet in formation. As it was, both sides were simply to let cannon play at each other for a few more hours yet, killing many men in the process. Marlborough had hoped to hear that Eugene was in place by 11 a.m. It was now nearly noon. He despatched his trusted quartermaster, General William Cadogan, to bring him information of the Prince's progress.

Newly married, in April 1704, Cadogan, 'a burly giant', was one of the principal organisers of the long march, and was one of the few to know its real destination; his regiment became known as the Fifth Dragoon Guards (now the Royal Inniskilling Guards). He was educated at Westminster School and Trinity College Dublin, joining the army in 1690 at the Battle of the Boyne. He was created Earl of Cadogan fourteen years after the Battle of Blenheim, in 1718.

Marlborough used the time to ride among his troops, giving the men, including Kit, words of encouragement. Suddenly, a cannonball landed within a few feet of his horse. His reliable steed did not flinch, and neither did Marlborough. Displaying no alarm, he walked quietly on. His adoring troops greeted him with cheerful impatience, eager to begin fighting, while on the banks of the Nebel, in the face of the enemy, the Dragoons continued impudently laying fascines and pontoons across the brook and the marshy ground on its far side.

15

The Battle of Blenheim

The sun blazed down out of a cloudless August sky. Peasants in their fields beyond the battle arena continued to harvest whatever corn remained standing and bound it into stooks, seemingly oblivious to what was going on around them, even as the Allied men began to ford the Nebel, which was shallower than usual due to the hot weather. At the Danube, the last local families made good their escape, with baskets on their heads and sacks slung over their shoulders; goats, pigs and dogs shared their boats with them.

The Dragoons dismounted and led their horses across the rickety bridges and the marsh; even then some of the heavier horses floundered in the boggy terrain. At last, word came to Marlborough that Eugene was in place. He ordered the trumpeters to sound the stirring chords signalling his men to attack.

12.30 p.m., 13 August 1704
Lord Cutts was commanded to attack Blenheim.

Simultaneously Marlborough ordered the central lines to move forward over the Nebel. The French centre ranks were not yet at full strength; had they been ready, they would surely have mown down the Allies as they struggled to re-form after crossing the marsh. Resistance, when it came, was full and bloody, but Marlborough had kept one step ahead of the enemy by mixing the cavalry with the infantry. As the Allied cavalry wheeled away, the infantry greeted the French with a hail of gunfire. That the infantry could stand their ground in the face of oncoming enemy cavalry like that spoke volumes for Marlborough. Orkney was the only commander at Blenheim to have two battalions of his regiment present, one in action and the other seconded to escort prisoners afterwards. When Richard discovered he was in the latter he must have looked skywards. Perhaps there was a God, after all.

1 p.m.
Brigadier General Archibald Rowe led the first attack on Blenheim village from the front but was met with strong defence by the men in the village stronghold; the General told his men they were to fire one round only, and not until he had struck the village palisade with his sword. After that they were to fight with their bayonets and swords.

196

They were now 30 yards away from the village boundary. Rowe walked forward and waited, and waited, and waited yet some more, even as shot was raining down. He marched right up to the fence and struck.

'Fire!' he yelled.

The Allies let off their volley, but Rowe was fatally shot in the thigh and slumped down. Two of his officers, Lieutenant Colonel John Dalyell, and Major William Campbell, ran to his aid, intending to carry him off the field; but they were both shot dead at point-blank range. Many more Allied soldiers were killed and the rest withdrew, reeling from the onslaught. It was not a good start.

A second attack brought a similar result. Now Kit and her fellows were called into action, to attempt a third onslaught. Had she downed her ration of gin? Was her grey horse fidgeting beneath her, keen and eager, like its rider? Certainly the air was filled with smoke and the noise of battle was all around.

Kit was among 25 officers and 315 men of Lord Hay's Dragoons, 'the Greys'.

They began their disciplined charge, meeting all eight squadrons of the elite French Gens d'Armes head on, and on both flanks. The dragoons remained steady through the smoke, trotting knee to knee, right up to the superior French forces. Then they unleashed their swords and slashed them to pieces. All the training that Kit and her fellows had undertaken paid off, and the Greys were rewarded with the first of their 'battle honours'.

Kit was to record, 'I received no hurt, though often in the hottest of fire.'

Later in the day, the French tried to re-form their famous unit, but there were not enough of its number left to do so.

Watching in horror and mindful only of his orders to save Blenheim at all costs, Clerambault panicked and, without consulting Tallard, ordered the remaining French forces outside the village to come in. The French reserve infantry brigades and their dismounted dragoons poured into Blenheim village. On the route march the French dragoons had lost almost all their horses, probably from glanders (also known as farcy), a highly contagious disease causing poisonous ulcers, abscesses and a nasty yellow-green nasal discharge. There is no cure or vaccination, but if the French had isolated and quarantined their sick horses they would not have lost so many.

Thanks to Clerambault's orders, upwards of 12,000 men were holed up behind their own barricades, in amongst the hens and pigs and farm implements, and there they remained, surrounded by the Allies and rendered impotent, caught in a trap of their own making, for the rest of the day.

Some of the Allied troops were drawn off to strengthen other parts of the field, the Greys amongst them.

Clerambault, who had made one of the biggest blunders of the war, eventually escaped from the village with his groom and two horses, and headed for the Danube; the groom's horse swam across with his rider but Clerambault's horse is believed to have shied at a cannonball shot, and Clerambault, who could not swim, was thrown into the river and drowned. The groom later said Clerambault, realising his military career had ended in disgrace, planned to live his life as a hermit; a kinder version was that he was reconnoitring an escape route for his troops.

2.30 p.m.

The main Allied body in the centre of the battle was facing fierce attack from the French, while over on the right, by the woods, the French under Marsin and the Bavarian troops were pitted against Eugene's forces; the two sides were proving to be evenly matched, with much loss to both, but Eugene's deployment there prevented Marsin's men from coming to Tallard's aid in the centre, another key point on which the battle turned. It was the Allied cavalry in the centre which eventually won the day. And still the fortunes swayed in the centre. Marlborough, ever attentive, not only listened to his messengers' news from every part of the battlefield, but whenever he deemed it necessary, galloped to a given spot himself to give his encouraging presence. Orkney, already opposed to the battle, did not believe it right for the commander to expose himself to danger in this way. But to soldiers like Kit, Marlborough's presence gave their weary limbs and sore souls the inspiration they needed.

5 p.m.
Kit would have remained comparatively safe had she been among those left surrounding Blenheim. Instead, she was redeployed to the centre for the final, decisive charge of the day. Marlborough marshalled the Allied cavalry into one magnificent line. The signal came, the drums rolled, and the massed ranks advanced at a smart trot, swords drawn. As they got closer to the enemy, the rhythm of the drumming intensified and the riders increased their pace in time with it. It was a daunting sight. Now, in the face of the advancing Allied cavalry the French cavalry

drew rein to present their guns, but scores of them were cut down on the spot as the Allied horse closed the gap. Those that were not wheeled their horses around and galloped away, pursued by the Allies.

In the rout that followed, some 30 Allied squadrons, led by Marlborough himself, drove the French all the way to the Danube. The banks were steep, and many perished trying to reach the pontoons that served as a temporary bridge, but not even this could bring safety to the remainder. It broke under the sheer weight of their numbers and scores of them were drowned. The men following behind them tried to scramble over the corpses.

One of those who had a lucky escape was Count Mérode-Westerloo, and his accounts of it also illustrates graphically the sort of hand-to-hand fighting that soldiers like Kit had to face. He accounted for the French defeat thus: 'For one thing they had too good an opinion of their own ability — and were excessively scornful of their adversaries'. He added that the French field dispositions were bad and that there was rampant indiscipline and inexperience in the army. 'It took all these faults to lose so celebrated a battle.'

Mérode-Westerloo was almost crushed along with many soldiers.

So tight was the press that my horse was carried along some three hundred paces without putting hoof to ground — right to the edge of a deep ravine: down we plunged a good twenty feet into a swampy meadow; my horse stumbled and fell. A moment later several more men and horses fell on top of me as the remains of my cavalry swept by all intermingled with the hotly pursuing foes. I spent several minutes trapped beneath my horse . . . everything happened very quickly, and the crowd soon passed me by; I managed to escape from beneath my horse, which was not dead but utterly exhausted, and extricated myself from the pile of dead horses that had fallen on top of us both. I had barely found my feet when a passing hussar fired his pistol at me. The next moment a huge English horse grenadier — a whole head and shoulders taller than I — came up. He dismounted and came forward to take me prisoner in a leisurely way. I noticed his lackadaisical air, and grasped my long sword, which was dangling from my wrist, keeping it pressed well into my side. When he was two paces I lunged at him, but I then discovered my left knee was injured, so I stumbled and missed my stroke. The Englishman raised his sword to cut me down, but I parried his blow and ran my sword right through his body up to the hilt. I wrenched my blade free, but as he fell he slashed at me again, but only succumbed in cutting the thick edge of my boot, which did me no harm. I put my foot on his head and plunged my sword through his throat. My blade penetrated into the soft earth and snapped.

Mérode-Westerloo's valet rode by at that moment, gave his master his horse and the valet was promptly riddled with lethal shots. The Count 'lost no time in riding off the way I had come, planning to swim across the Danube'.

He got rid of the white cockade from his hat which had marked him out as French and mingled with Allied cavalry, speaking whatever language was necessary to get him from one place to another until finally, deceiving two more Allied squadrons, he made it to safety in Hochstadt.

Camille d'Hostun de la Baume, Due de Tallard, who had been created Marshal of France the year before, did not escape. First, he tried to reach his men at Blenheim to tell them to retreat. Unable to do so, he made for the bridge himself. Finding that broken, he headed for Hochstadt; but before he could reach safety he was captured — a mighty prize for the Allies.

Tallard, astride a grey horse and flanked by two captors, was brought to Marlborough who by then was seated on his horse by an ivy-clad tree on a slight hill that gave him a vantage viewing point. The two men greeted each other with low, sweeping bows in the high good manners of the day, a scene that is vividly portrayed in one of the magnificent tapestries hanging today at Blenheim Palace; Tallard doffed his hat bearing a white feather in surrender to Marlborough. A stretcher is nearby, a carthorse is grazing, and burning can be seen in the distance.

Tallard was then confined to Marlborough's campaign coach; later in the day he was to suggest that he order his men inside Blenheim village to surrender, to which Marlborough pointed out that he no longer held any command to give such orders.

Tallard was eventually transported to Nottingham as a prisoner of war, along with a number of other officers. There, Tallard lived the life of a country gentleman, even introducing the cultivation of celery to Britain. He already knew the country from when he had been ambassador. With Tallard a prisoner of war and his army defeated,

Marlborough, still astride his horse after 18 hours, called for paper and pencil; an aide proffered the nearest scrap to hand — a recent bill of fare written in brown ink bearing the words 'pain, boeuf, chandelle' (bread, beef, candle) — and held up a drum for Marlborough to write on.

The Duke leant down from his horse and scratched a note to Sarah on the reverse of the receipt telling her of the victory. A messenger galloped off with the precious missive for the long journey to the coast, across the sea, and finally up the Thames to London, believed to have taken eight days.

7–9 p.m.
While Prince Eugene had wrought success on his wing, the French forces inside Blenheim village, unaware of their losses at large, did not surrender until evening. As late as 7 p.m. there was hand-to-hand fighting still going on and it was only two hours later that the Allies finally managed to persuade the French that they had no means of escape, and the French surrendered. The Navarre Regiment, mortified, burnt their colours rather than have the shame of them being taken by the enemy in battle; the thousands of Frenchmen inside Blenheim were taken prisoner and the village was set on fire.

That night, the Allied troops were told to sleep *in situ* on their arms, guarding the large numbers of prisoners; they formed a lane to enclose them. Even in August the night air could be chill and, coupled with exhaustion, the men faced an uncomfortable night. Kit was probably among them. Imagine their surprise and delight, then, when they found and occupied many of the French tents and discovered they contained 'great quantities of herbs and vegetables'; better still, they came across about 100 fat oxen ready skinned, which were to have been for the French troops.

Kit and her fellow men deserved their feast.

★   ★   ★

The official Blenheim Roll Bounty awarded Marlborough, as Captain General, £600 for his victory. The value of the bounties granted decreased as they were given to those of lower rank. Lieutenants, like Kit's friend Keith, were awarded £27, while 288 troopers, including Kit, each received £1 10s.

In addition, in the days following the victory, the men embarked on a looting spree as usual. Kit helped in breaking church bells to pieces and then, emptying the feathers out of a bed tick, she filled it with the bell metal as well as men's and women's clothes, velvets and about 100 Dutch caps which she plundered from a shop. Yet again she sold nearly all of it by lump sum to a Jewish merchant among the camp followers.

Of the battle itself, Kit wrote that,

Everyone has read an account of this battle which was as memorable as that of Crecy or Agincourt, so I shall take notice of one thing, in honour to that great and glorious captain, the Duke of Marlborough, which is: that after part of the horse of the left wing of our army had with difficulty crossed the rivulet, the rest also trying were twice repulsed which the duke seeing, led them on himself for the third time, and making the enemy give ground, their main battle was defeated.

Kit had come out of the battle unscathed, but she was soon to be in for a big surprise.

Among the Allied soldiers' duties was that of guarding prisoners. On one such detachment, Kit noted that the prisoners were the most miserable she had ever seen; some had no shirts, others no shoes or stockings, while others were 'naked as from the womb'. They were marched 'in this wretched condition' to the Plain of Breda where they stopped for refreshment. Every man, including prisoners, was allowed a meal of beer and a pennyworth of bread and cheese. There, a band of women anxiously waited to discover the fate of their loved ones. There was much commotion and raw emotion as some were reunited amid caresses and congratulations, while others who learnt the worst wailed and sobbed.

And Breda was to alter Kit's life forever.

16

Battle of the Sexes

Through a gap in a tall fence Kit saw a Dutch woman 'with a visible joy in her face make up to a man whom, by his side face, I fancied I had known; I drew near to the palisades where my horse was tied and looking through at the instant he turned to embrace her, had a full view of, and perfectly knew him, to my unspeakable grief, to be my perfidious husband, on whose account I had experienced so much fatigue, such misery, and had so often hazarded my life.'

Kit had much to say about this revelation.

Seeing him caress her so enraged Kit that she 'resolved to banish every tender thought which I might plead for his favour and wipe the idea of him out of my memory.'

She turned her back on them,

But had no sooner done it but I began to think of his infidelity rather a misfortune to me than a fault in him as he had never received any news or answer to his letters, of which he mentioned 12 in the only one I received . . . I was so divided between rage and love, resentment and compassion, that the agitation of my mind had such a visible effect on my body, and was so plain to see, that my comrade asked what had made me change my colour and tremble . . . I had a pot of beer in my hand and only had the power to utter, 'Take the beer, I can hold it in no longer.'

After a bit, she recovered enough to say she had seen her brother, Richard, of whom she had often said she had heard nothing. 'And there he was, in the foremost rank of Lord Orkney's Regiment of Foot, not seen for 12 years.'

Before she could speak with him herself the drums rolled and the trumpets blew, ordering them to march on, still bound for Breda.

And so, with Richard not having seen Kit, they formed into their ranks and files, leaving Kit and Richard about a league apart (approximately three miles), 'but it seemed like ten, so uneasy and anxious to speak to him and hear what he could say in his vindication'.

The last time they had seen each other, before he went off to pay a local debt, they had been so much in love, he the handsome and hard-working husband, she the mother of their two children, the third expected. But before she could hope to catch him again the prisoners had to be housed. They were marched into town and billeted in public houses, and with reluctant citizens. The moment she came off duty, Kit sought Richard. She went to the main guard and from there, in a public house just behind, she could see him drinking with the Dutch woman. Avoiding them, Kit sidled up to the landlady and asked for a private room, whence she repaired with a pint of lougarde — a white, whey-like beer — to compose herself.

Head on hand, elbow on table, and feeling thoroughly sorry for herself, she reflected on her former happiness, owning the Dublin pub, marrying the best man on earth, loving her children. And of the lengths she had gone to in search of him; and now she had found him and it appeared he no longer thought of her — yet, she reasoned, surely he was obliged to by the strongest ties of gratitude?

The battles inside her head continued. 'But have I done more than my duty? Is he not my husband? Nay, did he not, until an unseen misfortune tore him from me, treat me with the greatest tenderness? Had I once reason to complain of his want of love or gratitude? But why is he thus changed?'

211

At this point, thinking of his evident fondness for the Dutch woman, she burst into tears; they flowed freely and brought her some relief.

She cried for a good quarter of an hour before she drank a little of the lougarde; she then washed her eyes and face with the rest to conceal her having wept. Composing herself further, she called the landlady for another beer, and asked her to acquaint the young man of Orkney's Regiment who was drinking in her kitchen that she desired to speak to him.

Kit sat with her back to the light so that 'he might not see my face plain enough to discover me before I had sounded what interest I retained in his heart'.

Richard was ushered into the room by the landlady and Kit saluted him by name. He politely reciprocated but said she had the advantage in knowing him, but that she was a stranger to him.

'Yes, Sir,' she replied, 'you are not unknown to me. Pray, when did you hear from your wife and children?'

'Sir,' he said, 'I have heard no news of them these twelve years, though I have written no less than a dozen letters to her, which I believe must have miscarried.'

'Perhaps you don't mind, since there are a

number of pretty girls here who are all tender-hearted to gentlemen of the sword? They would easily compensate the absence of, and prevent any concern for a wife. You doubtless find it so.'

'Sir,' replied he, 'you take me for a villain, and you lie; I do not find it so.'

While trying to disguise her joy at hearing this, Kit nevertheless secretly owned that it gave her greater pleasure 'than if I had been complimented at the head of all our troops by the Duke of Marlborough'.

A sudden tremor seized her, which Richard, who by now had his hand on his sword, saw, and looking at her more intently, realised the soldier sitting in front of him was none other than his wife.

'Oh, heavens!' he cried, 'Is this possible? Is it not delusion? Do I really see my dear Christian? May I believe my eyes?'

He ran to her, clasped her in his arms, kissed her rapturously and 'bedewed my cheeks with tears of joy'.

Kit felt the old pangs of longing quiver through her but with great effort, as soon as she could, she disengaged herself and said coldly,

Yes, Richard, 'tis I, who have been so many years in search of an ungrateful husband. For whatever your sex may think of a marriage vow, it appears you never think of it at all, and the breach of it leaves the foul stain of perjury.

What a reward you have given me for abandoning peace and plenty, could I have known peace without you! I left my poor children, and my aged mother, friends, relations and country, to expose myself to the hardships, fatigues and dangers of a soldier's life, in search of a husband whom I have, at length, found in the arms of another woman!

Not finished yet, she implored, 'How have I deserved this treatment? What fault of mine, if not my over-fondness, could make you cruelly desert me and your children, and rather desperately take up with a life of incessant toil and penury? You drove your wife to the utmost despair, by the reasonable belief of your being murdered. It's impossible for me to think you could make so barbarous and ungrateful a return for my tenderness.'

At last she drew breath and Richard was able to speak.

'My dear Christian,' he said, 'do not embitter the joy I feel in meeting with you by such cruel and undeserved reproaches. Had you received any of my letters you must have learned of my misfortune which caused our unhappy separation. It was not my fault, and in every one of my letters I gave you a true account.'

'I wish,' she said, interrupting him, 'I had not received that which you said was your twelfth; for my tenderness would not let me believe you capable of a falsity, as I am now convinced you are; it was the fatal receipt of that letter which ruined my peace, by going in search of you.

'Yes,' she barely paused for breath, 'that letter made me resolve to undergo all dangers, rather than not find you out.'

Had it not come to hand, I might have been still undeceived in the belief of your death. Time would have mitigated my grief, and forgetting you, as I am a witness you did me, I might have continued at this time in easy and happy circumstance, have enjoyed the comfort of my friends and relations, and have done my duty to my children, in taking care of their education and settlement, instead of being harassed with fatigues of war, and my poor infants exposed to the hazard of being brought up vagabonds.

I have at length found you, but so altered from the just and endearing husband you once were, that I had rather have had assurance of your death, than see you thus survive your affections which I once was fool enough to believe nothing could take from me.

At last Richard got another word in. 'Believe me, my dear Christian, they are still as warm towards you as ever; pardon my faults, which I acknowledge, and make a just distinction between the tender, friendly love for a wife, and the slight, trifling complaisance for such creatures as may prove our amusement, but can never gain our esteem, and where that is wanting, you are satisfied, however it may be counterfeited, there can be no warm affection.'

Kit retorted, 'How know I that woman is not your wife?'

'No,' he answered, 'I own I have my follies, but that does not make me unjust.'

Just then there was a knock at the door. The Dutch woman, puzzled by Richard's absence, entered at Kit's bidding.

The woman said to Richard, 'My dear, why do you leave me thus alone?'

This evidence of her fondness threw Richard into a passion and he swore that if she ever used that expression again, or followed him any more, he would be her death.

But this did not impress Kit.

'Passion,' she pointed out, 'proceeds very often from, and is a proof of, guilt. It is not manly to treat a woman ill, especially if you have, as much I fear, seduced her with a promise of marriage, a practice too customary with our cloth. In such case I shall hold her innocent, if, when she knows you have a wife and children, she breaks off a conversation which will be then criminal in her to continue.'

Turning to the woman, she asked her if Richard was her husband.

When she answered yes, Richard again threw himself into a passion, denying, with bitter imprecations, his ever being married to her.

Kit repeated the question, and the woman admitted that the ceremony had not been performed, but said they had been contracted for several months and, when he was not in the field, they cohabited as man and wife.

'I am sorry for your misfortune,' Kit said, 'for this man is married and has been so many years, to my sister, by whom he has had three children; so that you can have nothing to expect from him but scandal.

'If you value your reputation or safety, or have any regard for him, avoid him for the future, for I have so great a love for my sister, that if he continue to injure her, I would revenge it as an insult on myself, and expose my life rather than suffer her to be wronged with impunity.

'What is passed can only be redressed by your being no more guilty; on that condition I forgive you, and will endeavour to forget it.'

The poor woman burst into tears. No man, she said, should have robbed her of her innocence, but she was betrayed by his reiterated promises, backed with solemn oaths, to make her his lawful wife.

Richard denied this passionately, causing the woman to fly into such a rage, and to vilify him in such 'opprobrious terms' that Kit feared he would do her a mischief, so she found herself trying to appease them both.

At last, through a mix of temper and reason, Kit managed to restore calm between them, but it did not stop the woman's tears. She left the room weeping and with a resolution that seemed sincere to Kit never to come near him again.

With her gone, Kit faced Richard again and 'represented to him, in the blackest colours, the villainy of seducing young women by promises of marriage'. She told him that he 'must account for the breach of such oaths in another life, if he escaped unpunished in this'.

Still she was not finished. She delivered her bombshell.

Notwithstanding the hardships she had gone through, and the wounds she had received, she said, she found she had such a liking to the service that she would continue in it. They could pass off as brothers, and she would furnish him with what shirts, or other necessaries he wanted, in return for him concealing her sex; but if he divulged the truth she would forget he was her husband and, she threatened, he would find her a dangerous enemy.

'What, then,' he exclaimed, 'will you be cruel enough to rob me of my wife? Will you not give me the satisfaction of letting the world know how much you deserve, and how gratefully I can acknowledge the obligation your uncommon love has lain me under?

'For heaven's sake,' he beseeched, 'reverse so intolerable a sentence! What! Have you run so many hazards, borne the fatigue of so many years, only to have the satisfaction of tormenting me? Do you call this love? Banish me from your bed — '

Kit interrupted him by claiming he had forfeited his right to it, by having taken another to his. She told him her resolution was fixed, and no urgings of his could shake it. And if he continued with, or at any time renewed his vain solicitations, she would never see him, or assist him again — unless peace or accident otherwise revealed her sex.

'Well,' said Richard dismally, 'I hope time will mollify you. I must obey.'

They sat together some time, and then she paid the reckoning and gave Richard a piece of gold, telling him he would find her a kind and generous brother, but that he must not think of enjoying his wife while her sex remained concealed and the war lasted.

He detected a hint of hope.

Embracing her passionately, he told her he did not think her heart as hard as he found it. They left the inn and returned to their respective posts.

Poor Richard: banished from Kit's bed, yet banned from the other woman's! Kit was a hard taskmaster. Was it really that her love of soldiering had overtaken her long-held love of her husband? And, given time, would she relent?

Kit and her 'brother' met daily for a chat, but whenever he began his 'solicitations', Kit immediately put a stop to them. Did she, in her heart, dream of the war ending, of God having spared their lives, and of resuming her business with Richard in Dublin as if nothing had happened in between?

★ ★ ★

For Kit the first part of the winter was spent quartered in Rotterdam, where the Meuse and the Rhine flow into the North Sea, but the Foot, Richard included, were left inland. Kit soon got up to her old tricks again. She obtained permission to visit The Hague, 'certainly the most beautiful village in the world', and befriended a fellow traveller; a young, pretty girl. Soon Kit, who was dressed 'genteelly, in a plain suit', was back in Rotterdam and showing the girl around the city: the Town House, the Anatomy Chambers, and the bronze statue of the town's most famous son, the humanist religious reformer and philosopher Desiderius Erasmus, as well as the house where he was born.

The pair travelled on to Delft, which she said was 'the worst paved town in Holland', and then to Amsterdam, where Kit 'gallanted my pretty frow [frau] through the street, said all the fine things to her I could think of, and was so importunate to know her place of abode'.

Before long she had inveigled herself back to the girl's house, where they drank wine together. When Kit came to take her leave the girl 'threw her arms around my neck and would have kissed me. I pushed her rudely off, saying, I had mistaken a fiend for an angel. I would have gone directly out of the house, but she clapped herself before the door, and told me I must first pay for the bottle of wine. I threw down the money, and flew out of the house in a rage'.

★ ★ ★

The 1705 campaign was about to begin, and as winter turned to spring and summer France gained some respite. Marlborough had hoped to finish off his successful work at Blenheim by invading France through the Moselle Valley, but once more he was thwarted by the Dutch who were unwilling to release their troops from their borders to fight elsewhere; he had to take a smaller army than he would have wished. And the French were proving unusually active.

They took Huy on 10 June, while the French were in a strong position along the River Moselle.

Located between Namur and Liege at the confluence of the Meuse and two smaller rivers Huy, in present-day Belgium, was first fortified by the Romans in the second century AD.

When Marlborough reached Coblenz he found that his stores there had been embezzled and the contractor had defected to the French. Supplies were so low, indeed critical, that there was a real threat of starvation to both his troops and horses, and on 16 June he was forced to call off his planned campaign, to unconcealed delight of the French.

Marlborough headed back towards Huy, which he promptly retook, and then broke through the French lines at Elixheim with barely a loss of life, catching the enemy completely unawares.

His chance of forcing open battle on the Moselle, however, was gone, and with it his aim of driving deep into France, to Paris itself and thereby a final conclusive victory. Marlborough's only hope was to strengthen the Alliance. He embarked on a lengthy round of diplomacy, attempting to gain more allies who would promise to fight with him the following year, 1706, as well as to keep those he already had.

So, although the Allies had also undertaken a number of successful sieges, 1705 proved disappointing for Marlborough. On the personal side, however, he was made a Prince of the Holy Roman Empire. It was a title he had been offered previously but had declined on the grounds that he wanted to do more to earn it. After Blenheim, there could be no further excuse for postponing this honour and he accepted. The troops were ecstatic that the triumph of 'their John' had been so rewarded, and Kit recorded, 'we were regaled with liquor and made great rejoicings'.

★ ★ ★

Marlborough feared that 1706 would bring dithering from the Dutch and reticence for a full-scale fight from the French. 'I have no hope of doing anything considerable, unless the French do what I am very confident they will not.'

But Louis would indeed court battle. He had had successes along the Rhine and in Italy — why not in Flanders? And Blenheim still riled with him. He was eager to avenge the French debacle there, and he goaded his commander in Flanders, Francois de Neufville, Due de Villeroy, to seek out 'Monsieur Marlbrouck'.

And so, just less than two years since Blenheim, the Allies prepared once more for full-scale battle. The theatre was to be back on the familiar flat land of the Low Countries at a place called Ramillies, some 28 miles south-east of Brussels.

At 2 p.m. on 23 May 1706, the battle began. Richard Welsh was still serving with

Lord Orkney's Foot and his 'brother, Christopher' Welsh, was astride her horse with the Greys. What Louis XIV got in return for his attempted revenge was Marlborough's most comprehensive victory of all. He again proved his great strength as a strategist in battle, leading from the front, and most of all by his ability to think on his feet.

Kit described the conflict:

The left of our army, which attacked the right wing of the enemy, met with a stout resistance before they could break them; which, however, they at length did, and put them to flight, while we were not less successful in the right wing. In a word, the enemy was everywhere entirely routed, and never victory was more complete. The shattered remains of their army fled in the greatest confusion, some to Louvain, others to Waveren, and the rest to Judoigne. We took a great number of prisoners in the pursuit, many colours and standards; artillery and ammunition, tin pontoons and baggage.

In fact, the French leaders, Villeroy and the Elector, only narrowly escaped capture and a similar fate to that of Tallard at Blenheim.

Once again, Kit 'escaped unhurt, though in

the hottest of the battle, till the French were entirely defeated'. After the battle, the Greys were allowed to wear the bearskin on their heads, normally the preserve of grenadiers, as a reward for their defeat of the Regiment du Roi; they were also rewarded with the second of their battle honours.

It was nearly midnight before Marlborough called a halt to the pursuit; he was near Meldert, some 12 miles from the field of action. The enemy was in tatters and reduced in military terms to a mere handful. Afterwards Marlborough wrote to Sarah, as usual. 'It really looks more like a dream than truth,' he told her.

★   ★   ★

Kit was riding back towards camp with some of her comrades, doubtless jubilant and full of the day's action. She let her horse drop its head, her rein long, but she remained upright, probably enjoying the badinage, the bragging, relieved that so few of her comrades had been lost. They were riding through a small town. Perhaps they might find lodgings here for the night, or even a hot meal. But any reverie was soon interrupted.

'Look out!'

Kit had not seen the stray shell falling from

on top of a steeple and her mate's yell came too late. It struck the back of her head. Kit was knocked to the ground, her skull fractured.

Lying prostrate, she was subsequently taken to hospital in Meldre, near the university town of Louvain 15 miles away There the surgeon took one look at her and deemed immediate surgery to be necessary. Her head needed to be trepanned. The upper half of her body would have been stripped prior to the operation and then the surgeon set to work. He used a small cylindrical saw to perforate her skull and he then removed a fragment of bone to relieve the pressure on her head. It was a delicate operation, requiring the surgeon's complete concentration. After it was over he leant over her to supervise the dressing.

Suddenly he exclaimed, 'Ye gods! This soldier is a woman — look, these nipples have been sucked!'

One of the most startling revelations of the whole war emerged. And the only battle it had to do with was of the sexes.

PART III

17

My Pretty Dragoon

Immediately the surgeons informed Brigadier Preston that his 'pretty dragoon' was a woman. At first he did not believe it. He visited Kit in hospital to see for himself and said, 'I always looked upon you as the prettiest fellow and the best man I had.'

Still incredulous, he summoned Kit's 'brother' believing, correctly, that Richard must really be her husband.

Richard said, 'Sir, as she is discovered, I cannot deny it; she is my wife and I have had three children by her.'

Soon the whole camp was buzzing as the news spread. Lord John Hay himself came to visit her when he heard of it, as did all her former comrades. Lord Hay asked her no questions, and would not allow anyone else to either, before calling first for her tent mate and then for Richard.

He quizzed the tent mate closely; he could not believe he had not known the truth; how could he not have known when living that closely? But the comrade protested he was telling the truth, that he neither knew nor suspected she was a woman.

'Why,' he said, 'it is well known that she had a child lain to her and took care of it.'

Lord Hay then summoned Richard, and the first thing he asked was, 'Why the disguise?'

Richard poured out their story: of how they had met and married; how he had come by mistake to the Continent; and how Kit had followed to search for him. He told him of what had happened when at last they had met up again, and Kit's 'obstinate refusal of bedding with him'.

Lord Hay was amused by this, and he at once ordered that Kit should want for nothing and that her pay should be continued while she was 'under cure'. What is more, once she was well enough — after some ten weeks — he sent her a parcel of shirts and sheets to make her shifts.

Brigadier Preston likewise made her a 'handsome present of a silk gown', and all her former officers contributed to furnishing her 'with what was requisite for the dress of my sex'. She was dismissed from the service — after a dozen or so years of duty — with a 'handsome compliment'.

When she went to thank her former officers before taking her final leave, Lord Hay had another word with her.

'I hope you will not continue your cruelty to your husband,' he said, 'now that you can no longer pass under a disguise.'

'My lord, I must own I have a strong inclination to the army,' Kit replied, 'and I apprehended the consequence of sleeping with my husband might be my dismissal; for a great belly could not have been concealed. The discovery of my sex has now removed the cause, and I have no objection to living with my husband, as it is the duty of an honest wife.'

In response, a delighted Lord Hay promptly arranged for Kit and Richard to have a new marriage.

Kit wrote, 'Accordingly all our officers were invited and we were, with great solemnity, wedded and bedded; the sack-posset eaten and the stocking thrown.'

Sack posset was traditionally a bedtime drink, made of sherry, eggs, spices, sugar and cream and warmed together. Other popular bedtime drinks were caudle and tansy made with similar ingredients, while a favourite cold drink was syllabub, made with fresh cow's milk and sweet wine.

After the ceremony all the guests not only kissed the bride but also gave her a piece of gold — in some cases four or five pieces — to 'put her in a way of life'.

According to Kit's account, that happened the very first night.

It is easy to imagine her lying contentedly in Richard's arms, totally at one with him. Radiance exuded from her face and her whole being shone as if she were 20 years old again. So this was why she had fought as a soldier all those years. What a day it had been.

And now she had conceived; she knew it for sure. She leant over and kissed his ear. He was already asleep. She fingered the gold pieces under her pillow; and she slept.

She also reminds us that, except for when she had been 'surprised' by Thomas Howell, she had known no man other than her husband. She was 39 years old.

★   ★   ★

While Kit had been convalescing after the Battle of Ramillies, Marlborough had wasted no time in pursuing the remaining fragments of the French army. He allowed himself and his men just one day off after the battle; the day after that the Allies began the relentless process of taking town after town, many left virtually defenceless in the wake of the fleeing enemy. One after another the previously impregnable enemy strongholds fell. With word of the Allies' approach having preceded them, they found Louvain deserted, abandoned by the enemy; Brussels followed shortly after and soon, within just two weeks of the Battle of Ramillies, the whole of Brabant and most of Flanders had fallen. Marlborough then requested the States Generals' blessing to attack Ostend. There was a very destructive Allied bombardment from both land and sea, and a hard, but short, fight. The port that had previously held out over a three-year siege now capitulated in barely three days.

* * *

Kit could not, of course, remain idle for long, pregnant or not. For one thing, she now had no income, and so she took up a post as a cook to Richard's regiment, which she adopted as hers, and returned to his quarters at night. But that work proved neither sufficient income, nor enough challenge.

'I did not long carry on this business, as the close attendance it required prevented my marauding, which was vastly more beneficial. After I had given over my cooking, I turned sutler, and, by the indulgence of the officers, was permitted to pitch my tent in the front, while others were driven to the rear of the army.'

It meant the men she had formerly been serving alongside and under were now her customers. As always she ensured she looked after the officers, but they now ranked second in her esteem to Richard; she determined to procure hot food and liquor and deliver it to him whenever she deemed he needed it, regardless of where he was or what danger he was in.

And that, as ever, spelled trouble.

★ ★ ★

Menin, a town on the border between Belgium and France, was another of Marlborough's targets. Because of its location it remained a prime target over the centuries, being retaken by the French in 1744; it was besieged 22 times between 1579 and 1830. The Menin Gate memorial in nearby Ypres, the subject of a poem by Siegfried Sassoon, commemorates the fallen in the First World War; the troops took the road to Menin out of Ypres on their way to the trenches. Today, the 'Last Post' is performed nightly at 8 p.m.

For Marlborough, 200 large and small cannons were brought, but although the town capitulated within 18 days, agreeing terms after a month, it came at a high cost to the Allies.

Kit recorded that 'we lost a great many men in this siege; I was myself exposed to no danger except when my husband was, whom I always followed, and whom I would never abandon, wherever he went.'

There was a sad loss after Menin in Kit's former regiment, the Greys. Marlborough wrote from camp at Helchin on 26 August 1706 to Robert Harley, Queen Anne's Secretary of State, reporting on the satisfactory outcome of the siege of Menin and his plan to move on and take Dendermonde, which would secure much of Brabant.

At the end of his letter he wrote that 'yesterday Lord John Hay, Colonel of the Royal Regiment of Scots Dragoons, died of a lingering fever, after about twenty days' illness, being generally regretted through the whole army'. The mantle of colonel of the regiment was immediately taken over by John Dalrymple, Earl of Stair.

While most of the troops remained to repair the damage at Menin, Marlborough's brother, General Charles Churchill, took a detachment of six battalions and six squadrons to reduce Dendermond; the town was almost inaccessible and proved obstinate enough but the town surrendered on 5 September.

Eleven days later, 40 battalions and 30 squadrons were sent to besiege Ath, while

General Ingoldsby's men, Richard among them, surprised the town by another way, losing only one man.

Kit was left behind, boiling her pot,

with which I designed to regale him and the officers of his regiment. When my meat was ready, I covered it with cloths so close that no steam could get out, and, venturing through a village belonging to the enemy, in which I ran the hazard of being killed or stripped, by a circuit of five miles, I got safe, with my provisions on my head, to the trench. It was a fatiguing journey, the way being difficult to find, and the night being very dark: but what danger will deter a woman who truly loves her husband? Having found mine, I set my broth and meat before him; he invited his colonel, and other officers, who were not a little surprised at the risk I had run, and that I could bring it so hot such a length of way.

Lord Auverquerque, who was come to thank the officers and soldiers for their diligence, stood talking to some of the former, when I, looking through the sandbags, saw a soldier, who, ignorant of our being on the side we were, came out of the town to gather turnips. I took a piece out of one of our people's hand, and called to an officer to see me shoot him; for we had pushed our trenches within thirty-three paces of the palisades. I suppose we were just then perceived; for the instant I killed the man, a musket-shot, from the town, came through the sandbags, split my under lip, beat one of my teeth into my mouth, and knocked me down. Both this shot and mine, with which I killed the soldier, were so exactly at a time, that none could distinguish whether I fell by the recoiling of the piece, or the enemy's ball. My husband, and some of his comrades, ran to take me up, and seeing me bloody, imagined I was shot through the head; but I convinced them to the contrary, by spitting the ball and tooth into my hand.

General Ingoldsby sent for his surgeon, who sewed up my lip, and took care of me in the cure. Lord Auverquerque, who had seen what had passed, made me a present of five *pistoles*, and told me, he was sorry that the pains I had taken, in providing refreshment for my husband and his officers, had been attended with such a misfortune. I stayed in the trench till the next night, when our regiment, for so I call that of my husband, being relieved by another, marched off. In a few days the breaches were so wide, that the besieged beat the chamade, [a drum or trumpet call inviting an enemy to parley or surrender] in the afternoon of 30 September, but all terms were refused them, and the garrison, consisting of two thousand one hundred men, on 2 October, were obliged to surrender the prisoners of war: the officers, however, were allowed their swords and baggage.

It was now October and so the fall of Ath marked the end of the 1706 campaign and Richard's regiment was quartered in Ghent. Set on the Rivers Scheldt and Lys, Ghent was and remained a busy port city with a thriving wooden and cloth industry, with many sheep raised on the surrounding wetlands.

During this winter, Kit's baby arrived prematurely 'which lived about half a year'.

That was the sum total of her writing of it, reminiscent of how she dismissed the death of her middle child in Dublin as she prepared to go in search of Richard: '(my second son was dead)'.

We don't even hear what sex the new baby was; different times, different values — maybe.

Soon, she set about earning a living once more; this time she was hired by the head sutler, Mr Dupper. She also noted with some surprise that the Dutch woman, Richard's erstwhile paramour, had moved into lodgings opposite their own, but Kit gave it little thought; after all, she and Richard were blissfully happy and the woman had promised never to see him again.

18

Domestic Drama

Kit and the cook turned out culinary delights and one day they had dressed a goose beautifully for a customer, a surgeon called Stone, ready for collection. Kit was in the back kitchen washing the dishes when Lieutenant St Leger from General Evans' Regiment of Foot sauntered in, saw the dressed bird, and demanded it for himself. A tall, strong man, he had, recorded Kit, 'a very handsome face and a genteel, easy shape, all of which he needed no-one to tell him for he had no small opinion of himself'.

This conceited young man was believed to be the grandson of Sir Anthony St Leger, a former Lord Deputy of Ireland between 1540 and 1556, but the lieutenant's actual parentage was of some dubiety: some said his father was a 'merry begotten' son of Sir Anthony's, others that his father and uncle were put in the charterhouse by King Charles II, originally a hospital for pensioners (servants of the monarch who had fallen on

242

hard times) and a school for 40 'poor' boys (sons of the professional classes rather than landed gentry), founded in 1611. Whatever the background of his father, this lieutenant was 'haughty, morose and vain'. He may not have lacked courage, but he nevertheless had a reputation as 'a bully, a gamester, a known setter and a sharper at play'.

Now, spying the beautifully dressed bird, he again demanded it.

The cook, a smaller man than the lieutenant, refused to give it over — after all, it had been prepared for someone else — upon which St Leger knocked him to the ground. Hearing the commotion, Kit came running and, taking in the scene, she collared the lieutenant, and in one swift movement she upended him by his heels and threw him to the floor.

With a crack like a pistol shot, St Leger's leg was broken.

Mr Dupper, Mr Stone and a number of others rushed in, demanding to know what had happened. Wiping her hands on the apron covering her skirts, Kit explained — and on hearing the cause, Mr Stone refused to set the leg.

Kit recorded that,

It was done by a French surgeon but after such a bungling manner that it was an eyesore to his dying day, no small mortification to him . . . His misfortune became a standing jest, for whenever he was quarrelsome in company he was menaced with me. Some years after I met him in the Tiltyard coffee house [London] where a gentleman asked if he knew me; he answered he had seen my face somewhere. 'Why,' said the other, 'have you forgot Kit Welsh who broke your leg?' He then looked more earnestly at me. 'D—n her, she is strangely altered, she is grown fat.'

' 'Tis true,' said I, 'in my person I am altered, but not in my temper; for, should I see you knock down, as you did, a man of much inferior strength, as was our cook, I might, perhaps, give you another broken leg.' He returned me some curses, which he could do as well as any officer in the army (for he swore a round hand), and left the coffee house.

★   ★   ★

We can imagine Kit, after this drama, almost skipping home to their lodging in Ghent, leaping over the dung piles and adroitly lifting her skirts and sidestepping the garbage like a filly at play. She paused when she was alongside the river and watched the little craft going about their business for a few moments. Beyond them she could see the belfry spire that stood like a sentinel on duty in the town centre, and behind it was St Nicholas Church; she must go there some-time, she mused, for the daily prayers and weekly services of army life were probably receding in her memory.

She walked briskly on, smoothed her hair, now grown long again, opened their door off the street and called Richard. He was not there, so she prepared the evening meal; perhaps the sutler had allowed her a joint of lamb. She may have added some sweet-smelling rosemary, and made a pastry crust with hands now light that only that afternoon had thrown a man to the floor. At length it was ready; she pricked it with a carving knife and the juices flowed and the aroma wafted, and she knew it was good. Still on a high, and longing to tell him about the fight, she called Richard again but as before there was no reply.

Venturing outside, she peered up and down the street. A smart pony and trap trotted by in one direction. She hailed an approaching neighbour.

'Have you seen Richard?' she asked.

The man looked skywards for a moment. 'Sure, I've seen him,' he said slowly, 'he's with his mistress in the tavern yonder.'

'He's *what?*'

But without waiting further the man scuttled in through his own door.

Kit began to tremble. Her whole body shook and she tried to curse but she was incoherent with rage. Hitching up her skirts with one hand, she ran blindly, still holding the carving knife in the other, towards the alehouse. She burst through the door and there, to one side, the two of them were sitting in a box, Richard on the far side of her, jugs of ale in front of them.

Kit's rage was so great that she 'struck at her with a case-knife I had undesignedly brought out in my hand, and cut her nose off close to the face, except a small part of the skin, by which it hung'.

Richard took one look, leapt over the table, brushed past Kit and ran for a surgeon, who sewed the nose back on. Kit ran for an officer who arrested both Richard and the woman. The woman's ordeal was not yet over, for as punishment she was put in a whirligig or turning stool. This was not the same thing as a ducking stool but was equally unpleasant, and was a common enough military punishment for misdeeds such as adultery. Disfigured or not, the Dutch woman was placed inside the wooden cage that sat on a pivot, holding one hand to her bandaged nose and with the other she tried to hang on to one of the wooden spars. The sergeant in charge gave order for the cage to be spun. Gradually the whirligig increased speed. People gathered round and cheered more and more as the misery intensified. She let go of the side as faster and faster she was spun, now both her hands were on her stomach but it was to no avail; every last content of her stomach was vomited up.

At length, the contraption was brought to a halt; but again, she was not yet finished with. Too dizzy to stand, she was frogmarched, a soldier either side of her taking each elbow, to the town gate. The crowds had likely swelled as word went about and doubtless amid great cheers she was ceremoniously escorted to the town gate, pushed through it, and with much clanking and creaking, the massive gate clanged shut behind her.

★ ★ ★

Richard was 'severely reprimanded' by his colonel and ordered to be confined. He must have rued his folly as he heard the cell door bang shut behind him and the key turn in the lock. Dear Jesus, what had he done? What had possessed him to go for a drink with her? Kit, he knew, was at work. What harm could it do? He must have paced up and down the small cell, repeating over and over, 'What have I done, what have I done?'

★ ★ ★

As the injured wife, it was up to Kit how long Richard remained confined. If she did not relent soon he would be forced to endure Ghent's own punishment: he would be stripped naked to the waist and forced to run the gauntlet of his regiment paraded in parallel lines, like a tunnel, each man furnished with a stout switch to strike the prisoner's naked back, chest, arms or wherever his cudgel should alight as he marched down the lane.

It didn't come to that. Kit relented. As she later recorded,

I own the violence of my temper, which is a very jealous one, pushed me on too far in this business, for I am satisfied, in the place where I found them, they could not wrong me; and, indeed, I have reason to believe my husband never injured me with women from the time I found him. To say the truth, I can tax his memory with nothing but an unhappy itch to play, which he could not be broke of, though it almost broke me, and was the only cause of uneasiness that I ever had all the time I was his wife.

In time the Dutch woman married in Groningen, nearly 200 miles away from Ghent in the north of the Netherlands, although their paths still crossed occasionally, causing Kit to be 'as well pleased as she [the Dutch woman] was mortified' by her disfigurement.

★ ★ ★

The year 1707 did not start well for the Allies, when the French stormed the lines of Stolhossen and gained command of the Upper Rhine, allowing them free access into Germany. Once more it put Vienna at risk.

Marlborough bade farewell to Sarah in England and sailed from Harwich back to the Low Countries in May, only to endure another season of playing cat and mouse but never being able to force a fight. In Kit's words, the two sides that summer 'did nothing more than observe the motions of one another'. Kit — now fonder of Richard than ever — found other means of occupying her time.

Early in 1708 the Young Pretender, with the backing of the French, made an unsuccessful attempt to land in Scotland. It made Marlborough more determined than ever to fight the French again. He was back in the Low Countries in May where he reviewed the Allied army, and then forced a march heading for the enemy; but in July both Bruges and Ghent fell into French hands in surprise attacks.

It was unusual for Marlborough to be caught short. Soon after the loss of Bruges and Ghent, he marched again, cleverly leaving his quartermaster general William Cadogan and his men to build five pontoon bridges across the crucial River Scheldt.

Thanks to this, Marlborough was able to get the 100,000 men under his control across relatively easily, to surprise the French who were entrenched among the hedges and bushes around a fortress town called Oudenarde, roughly between Brussels, Ghent and Lille. It was less than a week after losing those two crucial cities that he finally forced the battle he sought. Once more, the French were routed.

Although it was primarily an infantry battle, Kit made no mention of Richard fighting in it, but it is likely that Orkney's regiment was part of Cadogan's advanced guard. Kit does record, however, that

> The French were driven from hedge to hedge, and everywhere trodden under foot; however, they behaved very gallantly, and disputed every inch of ground, till, being taken in the rear by eighteen battalions and some horse, they began to lose courage, quitted the field, where they left a great number of their dead, and taking advantage of the darkness of the night, fled in great disorder, and sheltered themselves under the cannon of Ghent . . . We could not have obtained a more complete victory.

The onset of nightfall enabled huge numbers of enemy to escape instead of becoming prisoners, and it was this that prevented Marlborough taking the War of the Spanish Succession to a final conclusion; the war was to drag on for a further five years, the last two without the involvement of Marlborough after he fell out of favour with Queen Anne.

★ ★ ★

Within a month of Oudenarde, the Allies set out to besiege Lille. Before that, though, Kit was showing off once more, and this time she put her old riding skills and competitive spirit into practice.

19

Devotion and Danger

Kit was riding back towards camp outside Courtray, laden with provisions, just as Colonel Cholmondley was reviewing his troops. Seeing her passing by, Cholmondley, 'who was of a gay, lively temper and pretty much of what we call the wag' sought to tease her. Letting loose his horse, a full-blooded black stallion, it went straight for Kit's mare and tried to mount her. Provisions went flying as Kit turned around in the saddle and tried to force the colt's hooves off her mare's rump with her bare hands; in the encounter four bottles of wine were broken.

It was this that irritated Kit most and she chased after the colonel, throwing stones at him. Soon after, she was taunted by one Captain Montgomery of the Grenadiers in Lord Orkney's regiment, ridiculing her riding habit and joking about her mare and the 'amour' shown to it by Cholmondley's colt.

That did it for Kit. She challenged him to a race and the captain agreed. She put up a pistole towards the purse, and Brigadier

Godfrey put up another.

The course was chosen. It was typically flat land with a dyke down one side and perhaps a windmill half a mile away that they would go around, finishing where they had started. It is likely that men gathered around, ale was taken and more bets laid. Kit would have gathered her reins in readiness, her heels preventing her excited mare from wheeling round. The drum beat. They were off! Neck and neck they raced but the mare could not keep up the pace for far. She was tiring; her rival's bigger and smarter horse was still fresh and any second now he would draw away from her.

Quick as a flash, Kit rode her horse into the other's side, leaned forward and with outstretched hand pulled his foot from the stirrup and 'made a furious push at him, flung man and horse into a ditch, and thus won the race' — and the money that both sides had staked on it.

★ ★ ★

Soon all was movement in the camp as the army prepared to besiege Lille, a siege that was to last from August, the month after the victory at Oudenarde, until the end of the year.

Richard was part of a convoy that had to get through enemy lines to escort vital provisions to the Allied army. Kit, of course, followed him. Richard and his comrades were outnumbered by three to one in what became known as the Battle of Wynedael in September 1708, yet they managed to force the French to retreat, leaving many dead. Kit recorded that 'General Webb greatly contributed to this victory, which, however, he paid dear for by the wounds he received. I got a fine bay horse with silver-capped pistols and laced housings and pistol-bags. I sold my horse to Colonel Hamilton for nine pistoles; my pistols to Captain Brown for five crowns; and the lace of my furniture, excepting what I reserved to lace the knees of my husband's breeches, to a Jew, at five livres an ounce.'

So, in spite of her many masculine escapades and her love of making money, Kit was also becoming quite womanly once more, adding sewing to cooking and sharing her husband's bed.

★　★　★

Kit was out foraging one day during the siege when she found a chateau that had been abandoned by the enemy; she returned to camp with a large basket of eggs and presented them to the Duke of Argyll; she gave a number of cocks and hens to some officers. She returned next day and came back with corn, hay and straw for her mare. But she felt there might be something more valuable there, and she tried again on the third day, dressed, as usual for such forays, in man's clothing. The surprise she got was of the wrong kind, for a group of French soldiers found her, and took hold of her, her mare, and the feed she had so far gathered. They then began quarrelling over how to divide up her clothes between them. How might she get out of this predicament? Just then, the men's officer came in, and he turned out to be not only one of the many Irish who fought on the French side in that war, but a cousin of Richard's no less. She claimed to be Richard and after a bit of banter between them, was let free.

On her way back Kit's eyes were drawn to a glint in the hedgerows; suddenly she realised it was French cannons pointing towards the Allies. Hastily she gathered up the reins and galloped to the Duke of Argyll's quarters to warn him how close the enemy was.

The Duke was playing chess but Kit interrupted the game, spilling out her news in forthright manner. Lord Kerr rebuked her, and urged the Duke to ignore a foolish drunken woman who was not worth taking notice of.

'My Lord,' the Duke replied, 'I would as soon take notice of her advice as that of any brigadier in the army.'

He asked Kit her reasons and within minutes found her intelligence not only to be true, but that he scarcely had time to make it to the safety of the lines.

Kit recorded that,

Sir Richard Temple's and How's regiments were ordered to clear the hedges, and the Duke would have gone with them, and probably never returned, had I not prevented him by keeping back his horse; for both these regiments were cut to pieces before our horse and train of artillery came up, which soon drove them to the main body of their army. The enemy cannonaded the Duke of Argyle's quarters so soon, that there was no making a bed for him there; and he was obliged to take up with one of straw of my making, and Colonel Campbell for a chum. They had no candles, but I had two of wax taken out of a priest's house, and hung up one over their heads in a paper lantern.

Here they slept very comfortably, and

I took the opportunity to steal the duke's wine for the poor fellows upon the guard, who I thought wanted it to comfort them: I had left but two bottles, which occasioned the duke's butler making a great uproar. In the morning his grace gave me a pistole for my early intelligence, and at night I spent it on two of his servants, at a house of civil conversation.

Autumn turned to winter, but instead of going into winter quarters the fighting continued, for after Lille was won for the Allies, so Marlborough was intent on regaining Ghent. Richard was in a party of troops, as Kit put it:

a body of men under the command of a lieutenant, ordered to lay the ropes and to direct the cutting of the trenches: we seldom expect to see any of these return again; but here the danger was greater than customary, as the night was clear, and they were soon descried by the sentinels; but so remarkably expeditious were our men, that they were all covered before the enemy had got their forces together to oppose them. As I always accompanied my husband, however dangerous it was, I, as usual, followed him this time, but Colonel Hamilton stopping me, and saying, 'Dear Kit, don't be so forward.'

I lost sight of him; for the ropes being lain, he with his companions were retired into a turnip field, and lay flat on their bellies, expecting the trench, which the workmen were throwing up, to cover them. Major Irwin told me where he was; and both the major and Lieutenant Stretton begged hard of me for some beer; but as I had but three flasks, and feared my husband might want, I had no pity for anyone else; as the night was very cold, and the ground wet, I had also provided myself with a bottle of brandy, and another of gin, for my dear Richard's refreshment. When I left these officers, I met a lieutenant known by the nickname of A— and Pockets; a spent musket-ball had grazed on and scratched his forehead, which his fright magnified to a cannon-ball. He desired I would show him to a surgeon; but his panic was so great, that I believe, had he been examined at both ends, he stood more in need of having his breeches shifted than his wound dressed.

In his fright he left his hat and wig, but they being found and restored him, and he at length assured his wound was no way dangerous, he recovered his small share of spirits, but never his reputation; for he was called by everyone poltroon, and soon after broke as a coward. Leaving this Cotswold lion, I went to the turnip field, where I found my husband in the front rank, to whom my liquors were very comfortable. We stayed here till the trench was ready for us.

The danger was not yet passed and the next morning Kit was standing beside Colonel Gossedge when he was shot through the body. She at once gave him some of her precious beer and a dram of whiskey, and he gratefully promised her that he would reward her well on his recovery; but he died three days later.

The following day one of their drummers went out of the trench to answer a call of nature; Kit warned him that it was a dangerous place; he ignored her. Just as he had his hands in front of him buttoning up his breeches a cannonball shot away both his arms. None of the men would go to his aid so Kit, well aware of the danger, ran forward and carried him to safety. At first he did well under the surgeon, but he caught a cold and died.

Kit was to have an even luckier escape. The winter weather became worse than ever. Two days of incessant rain left no man in the army with 'a dry thread on his back, which was followed by so severe a frost in the night that a fire I had made before my tent, to dry myself and my husband, I ready believe, saved the lives of a number of our men. I burnt no less than forty faggots that night, which Brigadier Godfrey gave me leave to take from a stack in his quarters.' The night was so cold, in fact, that two sentries in another part of camp froze to death while on duty.

Kit had pitched her tent close to a deserted brew-house and filled her tent with the produce she took from its garden: she brought in so many potatoes, carrots, turnips and so on that she only had room to sit down in a small space by the door. Behind the tent she turned out her mare and an officer's horse. One day, while she was out foraging again, an enemy shot whistled straight through her tent, and out the other side, killing the officer's horse.

Not surprisingly, she deemed it prudent to move her tent further towards the Allied camp and out of enemy range. Once the Allies captured Ghent, Kit sold much of her produce to the hungry inhabitants, making 50 shillings.

It was in Ghent that Richard's regiment

was billeted for what remained of the winter, and Kit found work as a cook again, earning a comfortable living by that and by selling beer to the soldiers. She had been able to bring so much fodder with her that her horse cost nothing that winter. Yet, as ever, a 'comfortable living' was not enough for Kit and before long, in conjunction with Richard, the couple embarked on a successful smuggling trade. It began by a chance encounter.

20

Smuggling and Foraging

They heard the sobs first, then saw the hunched figure of a poor woman outside the town. Richard had obtained permission to go out of town with Kit that evening, and they had just walked out of the gate by the River Sas when they saw her.

'What's wrong?' Kit asked.

The woman blurted out her sob story. 'I have three small children at home and the only way I can provide for them is by running gin into the town.' She pulled her bonnet closer under her chin. 'But the excise men caught me the other day and seized it; everything was riding on it but now I'm ruined.' She bowed her head and began sobbing again.

Kit looked knowingly at Richard and he looked back at her. Together they escorted the woman to a nearby public house and there they laid their plan.

The woman had eleven bladders, each of which would hold a stoop (bucket) of gin. They filled ten of them with gin. The eleventh was filled with 'nastiness, which the country people keep in pits as the best manure for flax'.

Kit takes up the story:

I then thus divided the bladders; three I gave to my husband, two to the woman, the other five, and that designed for the officers, I took into my custody: three of the Geneva bladders were tied round my waist next my skin, two round my neck, so that they fell under each arm, and were covered with my cloak, the cleanly one I carried in my left hand, and though visibly, I pretended to endeavour to conceal it.

I went on in the direct road, but ordered them to go round a little lane, and when they saw the officers busy with me, to make a push for the town. I made for the gate; the officers, to my wish, perceived the bladder, and came up to me; I retreated, and keeping out of their reach, lured them away from, till I saw my comrades pretty near to the gate; I then suffered them to come up to me, who demanded my Geneva, laying hold of the bladder; I soon got it out of his hand who seized it, fell on my knees, and began a lamentable story of my poverty, large family, and sick children, for whose cure I had made a hard shift to purchase it. I amused them with this deplorable story till I saw my comrades within the barrier; but finding they were inexorable, and resolved to plunder me, I took my scissors, which hung by my side, and cutting the bladder, said, 'Since you must have it, even take it,' and flung the contents in his face.

One of his companions was coming up to seize me, but I showed him another bladder with my scissors, and he retreated, as 'tis probable he had an aversion to perfumes. I had now a free and open passage into the town, which I entered triumphant, with my bladder in my hand. I was no sooner in the town, but my husband and the woman met me; she was glad to see me safe, but when she found her liquors were so too, the poor creature wept for joy: and on relating my adventure, her laughter was as excessive, and had the same effect.

The success of this ruse soon led to them repeating it, but the next time, when the excise men saw Kit approaching they did not dare risk any repeat performance, and so before long she more or less had free passage.

When they saw her coming, the excise men called, 'There's the retailer of soil.'

Thereafter, Kit and Co. many times passed through the gates for the greater part unmolested; when a new officer was put in charge, he received 'so fetid a reception that I thought he would bring his heart up'. Their language was so provoking that Kit threatened thereafter to carry a pistol and blow their brains out if they accosted her again. She did equip herself with a pistol, but the officer did not know that she carried no powder or ball for it.

'However, as they had been told my history, I was so terrible to these poltroons, that I believe I might have kept them in awe with black pudding.'

★ ★ ★

The smuggling soon took a new form. Kit had raised a rough-haired water spaniel from a puppy and had him well trained to fetch and carry. Now Richard and Kit took him with them when they went to the town moat, where they lay concealed until smugglers came with horse-loads of brandy and other liquor in small kegs. They roped two or three together, giving the end of the rope to the dog; Richard called him from the far side, and with the rope in his mouth he would swim over, his long coat flowing like gentle waves; Kit would shear him soon and earn the three shillings that she obtained twice a year from a hatter. The dog was rewarded on the far side with a titbit from Richard, and then he returned to Kit's call, ready to repeat the process long into the night until all the contraband was got over. The couple's reward from the smugglers was three crowns a night.

★ ★ ★

It was during this winter in Ghent that Kit tells us she was pregnant again. Beyond the fact that it made her crave eels, it is never mentioned again; we can only conclude that she miscarried. As for the cravings, one Grenadier Hugh Jones, a secret admirer, left the town gates without permission — for which the penalty, if caught, was death — to satisfy her; he stole a number of eels from the wicker baskets in the moat and took them to her.

Pregnant or not, it was at this time that Kit found herself in man's attire again, to avenge a perceived affront. She tells the story of a 'pretty young fellow', a wealthy and fearless volunteer about 18 years old who resented the freedom Kit took with some officers; he told her she was very impertinent.

As Kit put it, 'The affront nettled me so much that I called him a *petit maitre*' and went home in a passion. She dressed herself in one of her husband's suits; she had bought him two 'very handsome' ones out of her capital 'which was not yet quite exhausted'. She put on her silver-hilted sword and went to the home of the young recruit's amour. Once there, Kit pretended to be madly in love with the young woman and promised her that, if she would cast off her recruit, Kit would not only marry her but also maintain her as the wife of an English gentleman of fortune.

The girl asked for a little time to consider the proposal and Kit said a small space would count an age to a man as passionately in love as she was. She would call back at 10 a.m. the next day.

Kit returned on time, the girl accepted and they spent the next three hours together during which Kit 'promised her mountains; a life which should be but one continued round of pleasure, and an affection which no time should have force to alter.'

During this time, the cadet tried to call but was turned away by the maid, which enraged him. When Kit left, he accosted her and went to draw his sword. Kit drew hers, and at that moment Richard passed by, recognised her and said, 'My dear Kitty, what's the meaning of this?'

Kit records, 'At these words, the cadet, looking earnestly in my face, knew me, put up his sword, laughed heartily, and taking me by the hand said, 'Let us be friends in the future . . . come Kit, I'd give you and your husband a bottle and bird for dinner'.'

He did just that, along with another officer, taking them for a 'handsome dinner' and a 'hearty bottle', and they were all very merry about the manner of Kit's revenge and became good friends. He asked her to undeceive the girl, and not long after took her with him back to England.

★   ★   ★

The bitterly cold winter resulted in a shortage of food, particularly for the French. Louis wanted to end the war, and negotiations to that end took place; it looked as if peace was going to be found and terms agreed had it not been for one point: the insistence that Louis should remove, by force if necessary, his own grandson from the throne of Spain. Instead, his subjects answered his call to sell their silver plate to help pay for the war to continue.

Marlborough, who had equally hoped for peace and, indeed, expected it, debated between besieging Ypres or Tournai, settling on the latter in June of that year. It proved a protracted affair.

One day during the siege Lord Cobham came into the trench that Kit and Richard were in; he ordered the engineer to point a cannon at a windmill lying between the trench and the citadel and promised a guinea to whoever could shoot it down. A soldier was about to try, but Kit snatched the match out of his hand.

'Take care it doesn't recoil on you or break your eardrums,' one Major Petit called, but too late. So determined to win the guinea was Kit that she put the match to the touchhole and BANG, down came the windmill. But down, also, went Kit with the recoil, to the mirth of the officers, laughing to see her on her backside.

'You're a bold wench,' declared Lord Cobham, and promptly paid her two guineas instead of the promised one. General Fagel gave her another, and four officers each gave her a coin for her troubles.

Soon after this, a Captain Brown arrived but just as he was mounting the trench his leg was shattered by a musket shot. The surgeon had no alternative but to cut it off; however, none of the captain's servants or nurses had the courage to hold the candle; Kit stepped in, and watched the operation intently as she held the candle. She was 'in no way shocked as it was absolutely necessary'.

The citadel had been heavily mined, and even when it was thought the place had been cleared there were sudden explosions, so that 'we often saw hundreds of men at once fly into the air, and fall down again piecemeal, or buried alive; and if any were dug out living, they were miserably shattered in their limbs, or half roasted'.

On one occasion a sprung mine blew up 400 Allied soldiers, she recorded, and another only narrowly missed decimating a whole regiment. Another incident happened by accident. Kit was out foraging when she heard a sound like a clap of thunder behind her; she turned and saw the air full of the shattered limbs of men. The explosion was caused by a spark from a pipe of tobacco which ignited a bomb, which in turn set off 50 sheds and blew up 24 men.

She describes the dire conditions underground. 'As I have often said, wherever my husband was ordered upon duty I always followed him, and he was sometimes of the party that went to search for and draw the enemy's mines; I was often engaged with their party underground, where our engagements were more terrible than in the field, being sometimes near suffocated with the smoke of straw which the French fired to drive us out; and the fighting with pickaxes and spade, in my opinion, was more dangerous than with swords.'

After ten long weeks Tournai finally succumbed, and Mons became next on Marlborough's list, but this, King Louis decided, was too great a prize to lose; he ordered that it be defended at all costs. The battle for Mons was to be a bitter one, on 11 September 1709, at a thickly wooded place called Malplaquet, south of Mons.

★   ★   ★

En route from Tournai on the 30 miles towards Mons, heading straight towards the French lines, Kit's eye was caught by a large, newly deserted house, surrounded by trees. Leaving her horse with a sick sergeant, who was glad of the ride, she ventured to the house and was not disappointed: there, ready for killing, she found a dozen fowls, a basket of pigeons and four sheep. She set to and killed and dressed a sheep, cut off a leg and trimmed off all the fat. She put the carcass in front of the sergeant riding her mare, hung the fowls around her neck, and drove the remaining sheep to their next place of camp, at Havre.

'Being here arrived,' she recorded, 'while they were fixing boughs for the disposition of the camp, and marking out ground for every regiment, I pitched my tent near a deserted public house, allotted for Colonel Hamilton's quarters; turned my sheep to grass, and hung up my mutton on a tree to cool.'

I then went into the colonel's quarters, over which, as soon as it was appointed, a guard was set; but by a bribe, I struck him so blind that he could not see me and my husband's comrades, who lent a friendly hand, carry off a large quantity of faggots, hay and straw for my mare and my own bed; fill all my empty flasks with beer, and roll off a whole barrel to my tent.

Having made these prizes, I cut up my mutton, laid by a shoulder to roast, the neck and breast to make broth; dug a hole with a hatchet to boil my pot in, which, the fire being made, I set on with the mutton and sweet herbs, and was enjoying myself by a glorious fire, when the army came up.

Colonel Hamilton and Major Erwood

came to my fire and were not a little surprised to see I had gotten so many things in readiness. I showed them my provisions of all sorts; upon which the colonel, suspecting that I had plundered his quarters, asked where I had got my barrel of strong beer.

I told him, that falling in with some boors [peasants], I drove them before me, and made them bring me what I wanted, to which he civilly replied, 'D — n you, you are a lying devil.'

'Come,' said I, 'you mutton-monger, will you give me a handsel [an inaugural gift, usually of money]?'

They called for a gallon of beer, and drinking a little, gave the rest among some of the men, and ordered the shoulder of mutton to be roasted, which I did by pitching two forked sticks into the ground, putting it on a jointed spit, and setting a soldier's wife to turn it. I made four crowns apiece of my sheep, besides the fat, which I sold to a woman who made mould candles for the men, and made a good penny of my fowls and pigeons.

To one side of the camp a body of troopers and hussars were reconnoitring the woods.

Rumour had it that they were filled with the enemy. The men were also charged with calling in the foragers when it was deemed necessary.

Kit was among them on her faithful mare; she left behind another horse, which she had recently bought, in an orchard and she also dug a hole and buried her money. She pushed further forward, against advice to the contrary, but had espied yet another promising large house. She was not disappointed. Obviously recently and hurriedly vacated, she found an oven full of hot bread, bacon and beef hanging in the chimney, three tubs of flour, two pots of butter and a basket full of cocks and hens. She emptied the feathers out of a tick to cover her mare to prevent the hot bread burning her back and likewise emptied a bolster which she then filled with the bread, beef and bacon which she placed either side of her, along with the butter; she held the fowls in one hand, put her left foot into the stirrup, and swung herself into the saddle.

Just then the cannon fired, summoning all foragers to come in immediately. Battle was imminent.

Left and right of her foragers ran; many left some of their plunder behind and in some cases even their horses. Kit scorned them.

'The fields were strewed with corn, hay, and utensils which they had not the courage to take along with them; nay some, whose horses were at a little distance, rather chose to lose, than venture to fetch them.'

Kit, by contrast, was unperturbed and stopped when she saw a fine truss of hay; it was just what her horses would need. She picked it up, laid it across her mare, remounted and jogged unhurriedly back to camp. There, all was in motion; nevertheless, she set about killing her fowl, fetched the other horse and retrieved her buried money, and only then did she strike her tent, and load it across the front of her horse.

At last she caught up with Richard at the rear of the army, but found him 'extremely melancholy'.

'This engagement will be my last,' he told her.

Kit tried in vain to laugh him out of it but he only repeated his foreboding.

Rain began to fall and as they marched towards their night stop conditions worsened, so that before long they were ankle-deep in mud. Kit saw the little daughter of one of their comrades struggling through it with great difficulty, and as she fell into the thick clay Kit scooped her up. By evening time the army halted on fallow ground within sight of the enemy, but as men lay down to get what little sleep they could — those that found the warmth of dung heaps fared best — Kit calmly rode off to another great house she had seen, taking the child and a couple of helpers, a butcher and a baker, with her. There, she led her horses into one of the rooms and dressed her provisions in another.

She made a great wood fire and dried the child beside it and then laid her on some straw. She now had 'leisure' (notwithstanding a looming battle) to go out and search for forage for her horses, finding flax, hay and clover. She made the horses a bed from the flax in their 'handsome parlour' and left them with the hay and clover to eat. She went to the well for water and was surprised to find the fleeing peasants had left the bucket there. She filled it with more than water, for with her various casts she drew up a brass kettle, a brass pail and a silver quart mug in a fish-skin case. In the garden she found and prepared some sprouts and added them to the pot of beef and bacon that was cooking in the kitchen. Beneath the pot, on the red-hot embers, she had potatoes cooking; a little of the bacon fat drizzled onto them; her nose wrinkled involuntarily at the delicious smell; the thought of a little butter added to those partly charred skins had her stomach rumbling in anticipation. But she would be the last person to eat; more important men came first.

Leaving the cooking to the care of the two aides, she raided the rest of the house. She searched from bare room to bare room, her footsteps echoing on the wooden floors, and 'found nothing worth carrying off, but what was too cumbersome'.

She turned her attention to the cellar and her luck was in. She found, 'to my great joy, a barrel of excellent strong beer. I immediately ran up for, and filled my pails; as I was returning with these full, I happened to stumble against an inward cellar-door, which, flying open, discovered another small one: I hastened up with my beer, full of hopes of finding somewhat better worth within the little door. I found two rundlets [about 15 gallons each] and two quart bottles of vinegar, and two more of very good brandy, with which I filled my flasks, and placed all my booty in the parlour, where my beasts were shut up.'

Now probably in possession of more food and liquor than anyone else in the entire army, Kit headed back for camp, having first fed the little girl and put more food into her apron, and having rewarded her two helpers handsomely. While she had been at work a thick fog had descended, making it difficult to see more than a few yards ahead, but at length she found the child's father 'very ill of an ague, lying in a miserable condition on a heap of dung'. Leaving the little girl, she searched for Richard; it was hard to see in the fog, but she finally found him asleep with his head on another soldier's backside. As word spread that she had food, the dunghills burst into eerie life in the gloom and Richard's comrades were soon tucking into the bread, butter and beef that she left them.

She woke Richard up and asked him what officers or soldiers he would like to eat with, 'especially such as he was obliged to'.

They invited Colonel Hamilton, Captain Hamilton, Colonel Irwin, Captain Ross, Major Maclane and Colonel Folks. Kit was doubtless warmly greeted as she spread out the bacon, fowls and sprouts before them; she gave two fowls, some bacon and beef to Richard and his sergeant.

But did he eat? Kit was probably chatting animatedly with the officers as these men, used to silver services, had to make do with their fingers. The recruits among them looked nervous; Kit gave the remainder of her provisions to them 'who, not being inured to hardships, were ready to perish with hunger'.

The mature officers, by contrast, boasted

confidently of another victory.

Kit had set aside some pullets with eggs for the general officers and she now brought these to them; once more her provender was warmly welcomed.

Did Richard watch her departure with longing eyes? As Kit departed with the rest of her fare for Lord Orkney she was probably laughing and joking with officers and recruits alike, her lithe body silhouetted by the light of the campfire. When she had disappeared through the mist, did Richard say quietly that 'she's unique. When I'm gone, she'll realise I only ever had eyes for her'?

21

He Would Fain Tell You his Master is Dead

'Come along, boy!'

Kit called for the spaniel again. 'Where are you? Come along.'

He was nowhere in sight. Kit clutched the beer that she had with her for Richard. Less than a mile away the woods were full of gunfire. Here, in the mile-wide gap between the two woods, the Battle of Malplaquet was being fought intensely; from where Kit sat on her horse, it was fiercer than any she had known in all the past 15 years of her experience; in fact, she could not even be sure that their men were winning at all. But still, she would get the liquor to Richard as usual.

He had still been asleep this morning when she went out to take food to the little girl When she came back, Richard and his comrades were gone.

★ ★ ★

John Campbell, Duke of Argyll, had paraded in his shirt before the men, to show them that he wore no more armour than they did. It could almost have been Marlborough himself as he spoke to them, and probably even Richard's spirits were lifted a little.

'You see, brothers, I have no concealed armour, I am equally exposed with you, and I require none to go where I shall refuse to venture: remember, you fight for the liberties of all Europe, and the glory of your nation, which shall never suffer by my behaviour; and I hope the character of a Briton is as dear to every one of you.'

Kit noted, 'To do him justice, he always fought where the danger was greatest, and encouraged the soldiers more by his actions than by his words.'

The chaplain would have led the prayers and given his blessing before battle started, early in the day of 11 September 1709, and Richard may have been among those of Orkney's regiment designated to manhandle six cannons deep into the woods. Certainly, the men of Orkney's regiment took the brunt of the battle that followed.

★　★　★

Kit entered the smaller of the woods with her fare for Richard. The noise of the gunfire and crackling was deafening, and branches and leaves were flying around in the smoke. Musket balls and debris rained down all around her. Twigs fell down her stays to her discomfort and she would have tried to wriggle them out with a finger.

She had heard that both the first wave of men and then the second had been forced back with prodigious loss; both Orkney's and her own former regiment, the Greys (now under the Earl of Stair), were prominent in the battle.

Prince Eugene himself was wounded in the head (and the French leader Marshal Villars was later to be wounded in the knee) but it was not until now, with the battle raging all around her, that Kit realised quite how bad it was — the worst she had ever seen. There was a slight lull and in that moment she heard her dog howl pitifully.

A soldier remarked, 'Poor creature, he would fain tell you that his master is dead.'

Suddenly Kit remembered Richard's foreboding of the previous evening. Dread filled every part of her body; but though she feared the worst, 'my hopes of finding him alive supported me'.

She turned her horse towards the piles of dead. She dismounted and, doubtless weak at the knees, began turning them over, one by one, nearly 200 of them. Many of them were

Richard's friends; his company had been decimated. Like an automaton, feeling nothing, Kit looked at more and more of the faces. Still no Richard. Was there a chance he had survived?

Perhaps she heard the whine of her dog again, this time louder and gradually she could make out his outline. He was standing over Richard's body, fending off a looter.

Outraged, Kit yelled at the man.

She 'would certainly have killed him, could I have laid my hands on him; for I was in so great a fury, that I bit out a great piece of my right arm, tore my hair, threw myself on his corpse, and should have put a period to my life had I had any instrument of death'.

She lay there for a while before the tears began to roll, slowly at first like the first big drops of rain in a coming thunderstorm; then they increased and merged into a torrent, and turned into a flood, pouring so hard with no sign of stopping. In her distraction she tore off most of her clothes.

She felt an arm on her shoulder. She did not — could not — look up, but through her sobs she recognised the voice of Captain Ross. He sympathised with her, and even cried a little himself, saying her grief touched him even more than the loss of so many brave men.

Apart from sharing in the supper the night before, it was the one and only time that Captain Ross came into Kit's story, but the compassion he showed her that day led to her nickname of Mother Ross, the name by which she became better known than any other then, and three centuries later.

At length she lifted Richard's body onto her horse and led it to a piece of ground where she dug a grave and buried him. She would have thrown herself in with him had not some of his comrades who were nearby prevented her.

Instead, nearly naked and without any weapons, she mounted her horse and galloped off through the wood. All she wanted was to 'wreak my vengeance on the French, of whom our army was then in pursuit, resolving to tear in pieces whoever fell into my hands: nay, had I had strength and opportunity, I would have given no quarter to any man in the French army'.

She did not care for herself. She did not want to live a life without Richard.

Kit had galloped almost as far as Maubeuge, some five miles away, when a Captain Usher managed to lay hold of her mare, and forced her back, or she would have 'infallibly been either killed or taken'.

For days Kit lay as if in a stupor in her tent, eating nothing, speaking to no one, and unable to look after her business. She cried continuously for days, and the only time she ever left her tent was to run back to Richard's grave, and scrabble at the earth trying to remove enough with her bare hands that she might 'have another view of the dear man, whom I loved with greater tenderness than I did myself, and for whose safety I would not have hesitated at sacrificing my own life'.

On every visit, she found the grave being guarded by her dog, but as she approached he ran back to the part of the regiment where Richard used to be. He also ate nothing for a week and pined for many weeks longer, being slightly helped once the camp moved on. When at last she was persuaded to eat some breast of mutton she was so weak that she fainted at the smell of it as she went to take her first bite.

Colonel Hamilton's lady (either his wife or his mistress), on hearing this, provided a more sensible broth which gradually enabled her body to take food again. She often thereafter invited Kit to dine with them; she also gave her some stern counselling. She gravely told Kit she was committing the sin of self-murder with her grief.

'Besides that, it is disputing the will of God, which we ought to obey with resignation, and not presumptuously call His will into question.'

On a lighter note, she chided, 'You oughtn't to grieve so much for one man when the battalion affords a number out of which you can pick and choose.'

Colonel Hamilton agreed, but he was pleased to see her eating again.

After about six weeks Kit began to get the better of her grief, but her business had suffered. She had allowed a drummer and his wife to look after her tent full of produce — but they consumed it all between themselves and those who 'came to sponge under the pretence of visits of condolence'.

Kit's horses, meanwhile, fared better than either her or her dog, having been taken in hand and fed and cared for by Grenadier Hugh Jones.

★   ★   ★

'I'll kill myself, I swear, if you refuse me again.'

Hugh Jones bent down on one knee and took hold of Kit's hand, imploring her yet again to marry him. Ten weeks had gone by since Richard's death but she grieved for him still. She considered the situation. Hugh Jones 'had often solicited me in my husband's time, but finding me entirely averse to even thinking of being unfaithful to him, he gave over his suit, and esteemed me for my honesty'.

My husband being dead, this esteem was changed to love; he now renewed his suit, and courted me for a wife. His care of my mares, his having ventured his life to assuage my longing when I was with child at Ghent, and his daily endeavouring to oblige me, together with his threats of putting an end to his life if I continued obstinate, prevailed on me to marry him in camp, about eleven weeks after my husband's death, on condition that he should not eat or bed with me till we were in garrison, which he agreed to, and kept his promise, however contrary to his inclinations.

So once again Kit was determined to keep up her manly pose in camp. There was not too long for Jones to wait, for the Siege of Mons lasted only a month and was won by the Allies towards the end of October. The couple began their regular married life in winter quarters in Ghent, which town Kit knew well, of course, but she says nothing of that spell beyond 'we spent the winter without any event worthy of notice'.

★ ★ ★

Marlborough and Prince Eugene arrived back in the Low Countries in April 1710. There had again been unproductive peace negotiations and Marlborough felt at a low ebb. The Allied losses at Malplaquet had been unacceptably high. He wrote to Sarah, 'I am very sorry to tell you that the behaviour of the French looks as if they have no other desire than that of carrying on the war. I hope God will be pleased to bless this campaign, for I see nothing else that can give us peace, either at home or abroad. I am so discouraged at everything I see, that I have never, during this war, gone into the field with so heavy a heart as I do this time.'

He got off to a good start, however, with a number of successes, taking the French lines covering Walloon-Flanders and a number of small fortresses and siege victories, followed by the siege of Douay; it capitulated after two months, at the end of June. The siege of Bethune followed; it too fell to the Allies.

In early September the Allies laid siege to

St Venant and while this produced another success for them, it did not do so for Hugh Jones — unfairly, according to Kit. 'My husband, who was unjustly forced to do another man's duty, being in the front rank, firing on his knee, received a musket-ball in his thigh . . . I was just then got into the rear of those who attacked, being willing to get as near to my husband as possible, when I saw his comrades bring him off; I was greatly troubled, but felt nothing like the grief which seized me when I found my dear Richard Welsh among the dead.'

Understanding that catching cold was extremely dangerous for a man with an injury of this sort, Kit stripped down to her stays and under-petticoat and covered him with her clothes to keep him warm. At first, all seemed well. Jones was carried to the duty surgeon in the trench, Mr White, who searched for the musket shot and then dressed the wound; he pronounced it slight.

But the next day, finding the bone to be broken, Mr White judged it likely to be mortal.

Once St Venant surrendered, the injured men were carried to Aire, where another siege was undertaken, from September 12. This place capitulated on 11 November and marked the end of the 1710 campaign; only then, finally was it possible to convey the injured to hospital in Lille — but it was too late for Hugh Jones.

'My husband daily grew worse, [he] had his wound often laid open; but at length it turned to a mortification, and in ten weeks time after he received it, carried him off.'

For now, though, Kit found herself alone in a strange town, with no job, no income and no contacts. She was no longer either in the army or married to a soldier. She was a widow again.

22

A Slippery Slope

The only person Kit knew in Lille was Brigadier General Preston and he, 'from a pure motive of generosity', allowed her a crown a week and dinner every Tuesday. In addition, whenever he was entertaining, she was allowed to take away any leftovers in return for assisting the cook, and this usually supplied her with three or four days' worth of food.

It was the start of a slippery slope for Kit, one that was to reduce her to living on charity, and to using her reputation as a soldier to beg for whatever alms might come her way.

As for the war, the outcome was not what might have been expected after so many victories. But for Marlborough, by 1711, time was running out. He had finally cleared a route into France that made it possible, indeed probable, that the Allies could march on Paris the following year, just as he had long hoped for. But while Marlborough now had an open path to Paris, the war had become increasingly unpopular at home; a sentiment compounded by the slaughter at Malplaquet, not to mention its cost. The Tories had ousted the Whigs from government in October 1710, and secret negotiations with the French began soon after. By the end of 1711 Marlborough had been stripped of his offices. The Allies were stunned by Marlborough's dismissal; the French, not surprisingly, rejoiced. By the end of the year Marlborough and Sarah had placed themselves in temporary exile on the continent; they were feted wherever they went. In ten successive campaigns against the French Marlborough had, according to Captain Robert Parker, 'upon all occasion conducted matters with so much judgement and foresight, that he never fought a battle which he did not gain, nor laid siege to a town which he did not take'. Kit recorded her own views: 'Nothing happened to me in particular all this campaign of 1711, which was the last the Duke of Marlborough made, to the no small regret of the whole army, by whom he was entirely beloved, not only for his courage and conduct, but equally dear to us all for his affability and humanity.'

The magnificent Blenheim Palace, in Woodstock, Oxfordshire, begun under the benefaction of Queen Anne as a gift from a grateful nation, was eventually completed by the Marlboroughs' own money. Marlborough himself did not live to see its completion, although the couple were able to move into one wing of it; it was furnished opulently, and includes the tapestries that depict so vividly Marlborough's battle victories. John Churchill, Duke of Marlborough and ancestor of Winston S. Churchill, died of a stroke on 14 June 1722 at the age of 72. Peace in Europe finally came with the Treaty of Utrecht in April 1713.

★　★　★

As for Kit, midway through 1712 she realised she had no future left with the army, notwithstanding that she had continued to maraud and cook. She applied to Marlborough's successor, the Irish aristocrat James Butler, Duke of Ormonde, for a pass to England, which he granted her, along with enough money to defray her charges. However, the officer from whom she was to receive the money 'gave me but ten shillings, which I am satisfied was much less than the duke designed me; for everyone, whether friends or enemies of his grace, will allow he was not tight-fisted.'

She travelled by waterways to Dunkirk, which was now in Allied hands and where her late husband's regiment was garrisoned. There she awaited a packet boat to England. She spent much of her time procuring what meals she could from various officers of her acquaintance, and once she arrived in London she stayed at The Queen's Head, a tavern in Charing Cross. From there, she set about trying to arrange her affairs; she was intent on securing a pension of some kind, or even a lump sum 'in consideration of my own service and the loss of two husbands in Her Majesty's'. First, she decided to go and see the Duke of Marlborough, although he was now both out of favour and out of office. Kit records that she

was very humanely received by his grace, who expressed a concern that he could not serve me, and gave me a gentle reprimand for not coming to England when he sent, and had the power to do for me. Indeed his grace was so very generous to send for me, before he resigned his command, which I forgot to mention in its proper place. I returned my lord duke thanks for the good intentions he had, and took my leave; at going away, he clapped a guinea in my hand, and honoured me with his good wishes.

Good wishes were not going to provide Kit with food or lodging. Frustrated, she decided to try the Duke of Argyll, who was still in favour with the Queen. The very next day she set out for his house near King Street, Westminster, leading off St James's Square. Before she got there, somewhere along Pall Mall perhaps, she bumped into him in his sedan chair. He saw her first, and asked his footman if it was not Mother Ross; on hearing it was, he stopped the chair and asked how long she had been in England and where she was lodging. He also gave her a guinea, but better than that, asked her to continue on to his house where he would see what he could do for her.

While Kit was waiting there, the Duchess of Argyll invited her to breakfast in her chamber and listened to her story; she already knew of the time Kit had alerted her husband to the enemy in the hedges, and said she would do anything she could for her. For the time being, she gave her one and a half guineas. When the Duke returned he made a joke of a 'dragoon' being in his wife's bedchamber, and he invited Kit to stay to dinner. At the end of the meal, the Duchess took her leave, kissed Kit and said, 'I know you and my lord will be better company, and talk over your camp adventures with more freedom in my absence; but I desire you will let us see you often, and be better acquainted.'

She was right, for after the duchess left 'we ripped up old stories, and were as merry as so many new-paid-off sailors'.

Before she left, at nightfall, the Duke suggested she petition the Queen for further assistance, and that he would support any such petition. For now, he gave her another guinea, and two of his aides-de-camp, who were also present, each gave her three crowns.

* * *

Kit, dressed in the best skirt, petticoats and corset she could find, approached the redbrick gatehouse of St James's Palace. She looked up in awe; it must be at least seven storeys, she thought, and then a higher turret on each side as well. Maybe she remembered one day in her youth, on top of the hay loaded on the wagon on her father's farm, and it had seemed so high.

She was ushered into the palace entrance, flanked on each side by full sets of armour. She looked up at the fine tapestries and large portraits hung on the walls as she waited for the Queen, clutching her 'finely written' petition in her hand. At length she saw Queen Anne descending the grand staircase. One can easily imagine her dressed in a gold brocaded gown with deep blue bodice, topped with an ermine cloak, and finished with dark blue slippers. The Duke of Argyll was at her side, wearing dark blue breeches, a matching rich silk coat with jewelled buttons, a colourful long waistcoat and lace cravat. They were deep in conversation but stopped when they saw Kit. The Queen smiled and beckoned her forward.

Kit fell on her right knee, as instructed in advance by the yeomen of the guard, and handed over her petition. The Queen received it graciously and helped her up. She promised to provide for her, and ordered a bounty of £50 and a pension of a shilling a day subsistence for life. Then, noticing that Kit was pregnant (the first time this is mentioned in Kit's account, with no hint of who the father was), the Queen said, 'If you are delivered of a boy I will give him a commission as soon as he is born.' She also instructed the Earl of Oxford, her Lord Treasurer, to give her £50 to defray the lying-in charges.

Kit thanked her profusely, walked backwards to the door which was opened immediately by a footman, heaved a sigh of relief and doubtless nearly skipped out through the gatehouse, feeling her future to be secure.

But the Earl failed to give her the £50, although in the end she got it from another source. As for the commitment to granting

Kit a shilling a day, that was not honoured either; without the Queen's knowledge, it was reduced to five pence. Only when the Government was changed, and King George I was on the throne, did Kit manage to get the daily shilling restored.

And to her sorrow, she in due course bore a girl, who, she said, went on to cause her 'great trouble and vexation' — but she did not reveal how or why.

★　★　★

Occasionally throughout her account, Kit remembered specific dates. One such had been the day her horse was cut by a scythe, during the Siege of Venlo, back in August 1702; another was Saturday 15 November 1712 when she inadvertently witnessed a duel in Hyde Park.

I saw four gentlemen jump over the ditch into the nursery, which made me suspect a duel, and hasten towards them to endeavour, if possible, to prevent mischief; but I could not get time enough, for they all four drew and engaged, two and two, with great animosity; one, who I found was Colonel Hamilton, instantly closed in and disarmed his antagonist,

299

General Macartney, and at the same time the other two fell, the one upon the other. These were Lord Mohun and the Duke of Hamilton; the former fell dead on the spot, and the latter expired soon after.

Kit was not averse to fighting with her fists herself on a number of occasions, usually when responding to a perceived slight when justifying her needs as an ex-soldier. Invariably she not only won, but also received money from any watching nobility. Indeed, she spent much of her time hovering outside the homes or meeting places of officers she had known, and usually her efforts were rewarded with either money or food, or both.

She also returned for a year to Dublin, where her mother, 'though upwards of 100 years[!] of age, travelled ten miles on foot to give me the meeting.

'The poor old woman, who had long given me over for dead, having in so many years heard nothing from or of me, wept for joy, and in such an excessive manner, when she embraced me, that I could not refrain from mingling my tears with hers, my transport being equally as great.'

The news from her mother was not good. Kit asked after her children and learned that the eldest had died at 18, and that the youngest was in the workhouse, the wet nurse originally hired to care for him having offloaded him onto the parish. She found that almost all of her furniture and effects had disappeared, or that those who now had them saw no reason to give them back. Only Mr Howell, father of the trainee priest who had deflowered her, was able to return her any of her goods to her, but they were the least valuable of those she had lost.

The pub had been lost to her, too. The incumbent had died and the freehold was claimed by another; given that Kit was abroad, this was not contested. She had no papers to prove her ownership, and not enough money with which to fight a lawsuit.

One day she saw Thomas Howell in the street; now a reverend, he was married with 11 children, but when he tried to speak with Kit she turned on her heel and entered a coffee shop; not long after, he committed suicide.

* * *

But the biggest disaster of all for Kit since leaving the army was her third marriage. After finding her pub gone, Kit took over the licence of another, put in a stock of beer and

301

began making farthing pies; she was doing well until a soldier by the name of Davies (she never revealed his Christian name) entered her life. Formerly with the First Regiment of Foot Guards, he had also served in the Low Countries but had recently re-enlisted in the Welsh Fusiliers. After their marriage, Kit continued to run the pub until he was posted to England, and she followed him as soon as she had disposed of her effects.

She took up her same trade in a public house in Willow-walk, Tothill-fields, Westminster and did so well that she was soon able to purchase 'at large expense' a discharge for her husband, but this was 'just so much money thrown away; for in two days after his arrival in town, being in drink, he enlisted in the guards'.

She took over a sutler's tent in a camp in Hyde Park, and there she once again begged money from the officers and nobility 'without which I must either have perished, or gone upon the parish'.

But she was taken ill; a high fever, and days of paroxysms, gave her no alternative but to give up the tent. The eternal hope of finding help from her husband was forlorn. 'As to any assistance from my husband, it would have been the highest of folly to have expected it, as he always spent more than he got; nay, so inconsiderate was he, that the day after I left the camp, he sold my tent and everything in it for forty shillings, though the tent alone cost me fifty; and, notwithstanding the condition I was in, spent every penny of the money.'

While she was laid up she heard of Marlborough's death.

I was greatly indebted to his grace's goodness, both abroad and at home . . . he had been my colonel, general, and benefactor, and the remembrance of what I owe to his humanity, will make me lament his death to the day of my own. I was, at the time of his funeral, well enough to go abroad, though very weak; however, I went to the late duke's house, and, placing myself by my husband, marched in the funeral procession, with a heavy heart and streaming eyes.

Kit next settled in Windsor where she lived off the benevolence of the aristocracy, but after a year she grew tired of so inactive a life and moved on to another public house, this time in Paddington; once more she threw herself into the trade and her business expanded. While there, she got some friends to request her husband's discharge from the army, thinking he might help her with the now thriving business. Some chance! He was as extravagant with money as ever, so that in no time Kit had to sell everything once more.

She returned to Ireland again but stayed only a year before moving to her husband's home town of Chester, where she lived for three years. She then returned to Chelsea, getting her husband into the 'college' as a sergeant.

Here Kit's account is at variance regarding dates again. The War Office records list a 'grant of Chelsea pension to woman who served as soldier within Flanders, 1717'. G. R. Gleig in 1838 quoted her admission from a 'list of old admissions into Chelsea Hospital' as '19th November, 1717. Stair's Dragoons, Catherine Welsh, a fatt jolly-breast woman, received several wounds in the service, in the habit of a man; from the 19th July 1717'.

Yet according to her account Kit had since 1712 spent two separate years in Ireland and three in Chester, plus a year in Windsor and some time running pubs in Westminster and Paddington, and also a sutler's tent in Hyde Park. She attended the Duke of Marlborough's funeral in 1722; as according to records she was already in the Chelsea

Hospital at that time, then the dates (but not her account of them) could just about tally at a pinch.

In its present form, Chelsea Hospital dates from 1695 and was designed by Sir Christopher Wren; in those days it was surrounded by hayfields, some distance from Chelsea village. It was originally established as a home for military personnel, and today the Royal Hospital, Chelsea, remains a retirement home and nursing home for those unable to remain on active service. Dressed in their red uniforms, the Pensioners are a familiar sight on the streets of Chelsea. They are also always seen at the annual November service of remembrance at the Cenotaph, Whitehall, and mingling at the Chelsea Flower Show held each spring in the magnificent 66 acres surrounding their home.

★   ★   ★

Kit remained a Chelsea Pensioner for the rest of her life, despite the fact that women have only been officially admitted since 2009. When Kit was there, the college was under the governorship of Lieutenant General William Evans, who had succeeded Marlborough's nephew, Lieutenant General Charles Churchill in the post. Kit cared for her indolent husband, despite being increasingly beset by ailments, including dropsy and scurvy.

The question of money stayed with her right until the end; the last lines of her account say she 'subsisted by the benevolence of the quality and gentry of the court, whither I go twice a week; but the expense of coach hire, as both my lameness and age increase, for I cannot walk ten yards without help, is a terrible tax upon their charity, and at the same time, many of my friends no longer going to court, my former subsistence is greatly diminished from what it was.'

When she had been in the army and then later following it, Kit had made a good living, and used her abundant guile fearlessly. We have twice heard that she put on weight when she returned to England, and towards the end of her life she had lost all of her former mobility and dash. Her dissolute third husband caused her more woes in her later life than anyone or anything else.

But she retained her sense of marital duty, and in July 1739 she was staying up night after night tending her husband who was ill. She caught a cold herself; it turned to fever and four days later, on 7 July 1739, Kit died; she was 72.

Although many reports give her burial as being in the grounds of Chelsea Pensioners

Hospital, it is not recorded there, nor is it in the nearby cemetery of St Margaret's, Westminster. Wherever it was, she was undoubtedly accorded military honours.

Christian — Kit — Cavenaugh/Welsh/Jones/Davies is remembered three centuries after her death simply as Mother Ross. She was a remarkable woman and, even accounting for exaggeration, discrepancies in dates, and in places figments of imagination, the life that she recorded was an extraordinary one.

The Battle of Blenheim

ROBERT SOUTHEY (1774–1843)

It was a summer evening,
Old Kaspar's work was done,
And he before his cottage door
Was sitting in the sun,
And by him sported on the green
His little grandchild Wilhelmine.

She saw her brother Peterkin
Roll something large and round
Which he beside the rivulet
In playing there had found;
He came to ask what he had found,
That was so large, and smooth, and round.

Old Kaspar took it from the boy,
Who stood expectant by;
And then the old man shook his head,
And with a natural sigh,
' 'Tis some poor fellow's skull,' said he,
'Who fell in the great victory.

'I find them in the garden,
For there's many here about;

And often when I go to plough,
The ploughshare turns them out!
For many thousand men,' said he,
'Were slain in that great victory.'

'Now tell us what 'twas all about,'
Young Peterkin, he cries;
And little Wilhelmine looks up
With wonder-waiting eyes;
'Now tell us all about the war,
And what they fought each other for.'

'It was the English,' Kaspar cried,
'Who put the French to rout;
But what they fought each other for
I could not well make out;
But everybody said,' quoth he,
'That 'twas a famous victory.

'My father lived at Blenheim then,
Yon little stream hard by;
They burnt his dwelling to the ground,
And he was forced to fly;
So with his wife and child he fled,
Nor had he where to rest his head.

'With fire and sword the country round
Was wasted far and wide,
And many a childing mother then,
And new-born baby died;

But things like that, you know, must be
At every famous victory.

'They said it was a shocking sight
After the field was won;
For many thousand bodies here
Lay rotting in the sun;
But things like that, you know, must be
After a famous victory.

'Great praise the Duke of Marlbro' won,
And our good Prince Eugene.'
'Why, 'twas a very wicked thing!'
Said little Wilhelmine.
'Nay . . . nay . . . my little girl,' quoth he,
'It was a famous victory.

'And everybody praised the Duke
Who this great fight did win.'
'But what good came of it at last?'
Quoth little Peterkin.
'Why, that I cannot tell,' said he,
'But 'twas a famous victory.'

We do hope that you have enjoyed reading this large print book.

Did you know that all of our titles are available for purchase?

We publish a wide range of high quality large print books including:
Romances, Mysteries, Classics
General Fiction
Non Fiction and Westerns

Special interest titles available in large print are:
The Little Oxford Dictionary
Music Book
Song Book
Hymn Book
Service Book

Also available from us courtesy of Oxford University Press:
Young Readers' Dictionary
(large print edition)
Young Readers' Thesaurus
(large print edition)

For further information or a free brochure, please contact us at:
Ulverscroft Large Print Books Ltd.,
The Green, Bradgate Road, Anstey,
Leicester, LE7 7FU, England.
Tel: (00 44) 0116 236 4325
Fax: (00 44) 0116 234 0205

Other titles published by
The House of Ulverscroft:

TWO TURTLE DOVES

Alex Monroe

Growing up in 1970s Suffolk, in a crumbling giant of a house with wild, tangled gardens, Alex Monroe was left to wreak havoc by invention. Without visible parental influence, he made nature into his world. Creation became a compulsion, whether it was go-carts and guns, crossbows and booby-traps, boats, bikes or scooters. And then it was jewellery . . . From daredevil Raleigh bike antics and inter-schoolboy warfare, to the delicacies of dress-making and the most intricate metalsmithery, *Two Turtle Doves* traces the intimate journey of how an idea is transformed from a fleeting thought into an exquisite piece of jewellery.

THE LAST ENEMY

Richard Hillary

Richard Hillary was a dashing and handsome young man 'with all the luck' who enjoyed a privileged life in the Oxbridge culture of the 1930s. He trained as an RAF Spitfire pilot in World War II and was shot down in the Battle of Britain, unable to quickly escape from his burning aircraft and suffering extensive burns. In *The Last Enemy*, Hillary traces his extraordinary journey of recovery, which included undergoing pioneering plastic surgery to rebuild his face and hands. It was first published in 1942, just seven months before his untimely death in a second plane crash.

MUM'S LIST

St John Greene and Rachel Murphy

On her deathbed, Kate Greene's only concern was for her two little boys, Reef and Finn, and her loving husband, Singe. She knew she'd be leaving them behind very soon. Over her last few days, Kate created Mum's List to help the man she loved provide the best life for their boys after she was gone. It wasn't the first time Singe and Kate had faced the spectre of death. Four years earlier, doctors discovered a large lump in baby Reef's abdomen. Kate, pregnant with Finn, was so distressed that she gave birth dangerously early. Afterwards, Kate received the diagnosis that every woman dreads . . .